Another title from Jossey-Bass
and the League of Women Voters

A Voice of Our Own:
Leading American Women Celebrate the Right to Vote
edited by Nancy M. Neuman

TRUE TO OURSELVES

In Celebration of Bella Abzug (1920–1998)
for Making a Difference

TRUE TO OURSELVES

A CELEBRATION OF WOMEN MAKING A DIFFERENCE

Edited by Nancy M. Neuman

Foreword by Becky Cain, President
League of Women Voters of the United States

JOSSEY-BASS PUBLISHERS
SAN FRANCISCO

Jossey-Bass books and products are available through most bookstores. To contact Jossey-Bass directly, call (888) 378–2537, fax to (800) 605–2665, or visit our website at www.josseybass.com.

Substantial discounts on bulk quantities of Jossey-Bass books are available to corporations, professional associations, and other organizations. For details and discount information, contact the special sales department at Jossey-Bass.

For sales outside the United States, please contact your local Simon & Schuster International Office.

Manufactured in the United States of America

Interior design by Paula Schlosser

Photography credits are on page 247.

LIBRARY OF CONGRESS CATALOGING-IN-PUBLICATION DATA

True to ourselves : a celebration of women making a difference / edited by Nancy M. Neuman.
    p. cm.
    Includes index.
    ISBN 0-7879-4175-1 (cloth : alk. paper)
    1. Women—United States—Biography. 2. Women—United States—History. I. Neuman, Nancy M., date.
    HQ1412 .T78 1998
    305.4'092'273—ddc21

98-25436

HB Printing   10 9 8 7 6 5 4 3 2 1   FIRST EDITION

CONTENTS

New Directions

FOREWORD

❦

THE LEAGUE OF WOMEN VOTERS is proud to be a part of this
remarkable book in celebration of American women. The essays collectively reveal the good and the bad, the flaws and the incredible strengths, of the American community. The women who
share their stories have encountered that community on an intense
and personal level, and they have changed it for the better. Some
have faced daunting odds and crushing rejection—all have chosen to
use their energy to make their world a better place. They are exceptional women who have accomplished exceptional things, but they
also are "everyday people," whom we can easily recognize from our
own lives.

Although each of the contributors to *True to Ourselves* tells a
uniquely powerful story, together they stand for the scores of heroines and heroes across the country who quietly, often anonymously,
choose to make a positive contribution to their community. These
are the Americans who really do believe in "we, the people," who
strive to use their challenges and opportunities to add, rather than
subtract, value in their own lives and the lives of those around them.

This year marks the 150th anniversary of the first Women's
Rights Convention in Seneca Falls, New York. The women speaking
to us from *True to Ourselves* acknowledge and celebrate those who
went before them and brought them to the very doors they needed
to open. It is important that we, in turn, now praise and celebrate
these women on behalf of those who will follow and will benefit,

perhaps unknowingly, from the trials they have faced and victories they have won.

The League is grateful to Nancy Neuman, League of Women Voters national president from 1986 to 1990 and lecturer and writer on women in politics, for conceiving and editing this collection of thought-provoking essays, as well as its predecessor, *A Voice of Our Own: Leading American Women Celebrate the Right to Vote.*

The League of Women Voters is committed to the value of participation in public life. We believe that making democracy work is the day-in and day-out obligation of each one of us. The measure of our society depends on us. Our future as a democracy depends on us. We can find no finer models and teachers of what it can and should mean to be an American than the women who have contributed to this book.

June 1998   Becky Cain
                                      President
                                      League of Women Voters
                                      of the United States
                                      1992–1998

PREFACE

❧

*T*RUE TO OURSELVES: *A Celebration of Women Making a Differ-ence* is a unique collection of essays, written by a diverse group of women who are actively engaged in changing the world around them. It tells the stories of real people whose dreams and disappointments may not be so different from our own. Each author explains how she has sought solutions to problems or followed her aspirations, providing readers with models they can adapt for themselves.

Each individual, in our opinion, illustrates the central theme of the book: that the true measure of a woman is in her day-to-day commitment to something larger than herself. *True to Ourselves* is an exceptional portrait of the immense influence and expanding power of women in American public life during the second half of the twentieth century.

Every woman in this book has experienced a merging of her public and private life in the cause of protecting and nourishing those things she values most: her family, her community, her country, and her integrity. In the course of their journeys, these women have been confronted with choices that tested their principles and ethics. In her own way, each has discovered the meaning of being true to herself.

A Commitment to America's Promise

True to Ourselves is a cross-generational expression of external influences that shaped women's lives in the late twentieth century. In different ways and at different times, the women's movement and the nation's civil rights struggles affected each writer and thus became an essential component of this book.

The impact of both movements is woven into the life experiences of the women in *True to Ourselves*. Several women recount the effect of race and sex discrimination on their lives and the tools they used to conquer both. At least half are the "first" in a particular endeavor, a phenomenon that is continuing, even though many people assume women long ago integrated every facet of American life.

Several contributors offer the perspective of women a generation after the activists of the 1960s and 1970s. Their opportunities, choices, and politics were shaped by feminists who came before them. Their aspirations expanded in hearing the messages of hope, opportunity, and equality spoken by leaders like Martin Luther King Jr., Cesar Chavez, and Robert Kennedy. But their optimism was shaken by the Vietnam War and the assassinations of King and Kennedy in 1968.

All the authors describe full lives combining family, career, and a commitment to public life, and share their concerns about a persistent backlash against the promise of the women's and civil rights movements. A recurrent theme is a call for every American to work toward a diverse, inclusive society in the twenty-first century.

Turning Points

Every life has turning points, positive and negative, that open up new visions of ourselves and steer us in new directions. We invited each contributor to consider an important turning point in her life that set her on a particular path.

These turning points are intensely personal experiences that have molded the individual in the past and continue to guide her in the present. If, as feminists claim, the personal is the political, the turning points in this book prove the point. The poignancy of these special moments will provoke a range of emotions in the reader, from tears, to anger, to a renewed motivation for political activism.

Most of the authors describe the influence of parents, grandparents, or significant childhood events in shaping their character, beliefs, and enduring commitment to something larger than themselves. Scholars characterize the way young people develop these values as *socialization*. Students of socialization will discover example after example of the phenomenon in this book. Most important, *True to Ourselves* offers them an opportunity to follow the process through adulthood in the stories of real women, and ascertain how each has applied her standards and principles to actual situations.

Honorable Lives

At a time of low voter turnout, high public cynicism, and a decline in civic participation, the League of Women Voters envisioned this book to stimulate interest in public involvement and teach by example. As a result, we recruited women who we believe have made special contributions to the community we all share as Americans.

As the editor of *True to Ourselves,* I hope this collection will inspire each reader to believe she or he can make a difference by getting involved in something that matters. In particular, I want the stories of these women to kindle the idealism of young women and men who are just beginning to consider their obligations to society.

My goal is to illustrate that a life worth living is a life of service to others—in the community, at home, and at work. The contributors to this book, in their own special ways, have been enriched beyond their dreams by their involvement, even if, for some, it has been thrust upon them by circumstance or tragedy. Their stories teach us that an accomplished, honorable public life typically is grounded in something very private: a strong ethical core.

We are very grateful that the contributors to *True to Ourselves* have been so willing to tell their stories for this collection. It is not easy to reveal your private thoughts, struggles, and dreams, even to a close friend or relative. How many of us wish our mothers and grandmothers, fathers and grandfathers, had shared these intimate parts of their personalities and lives with us? Or wish we had listened when they tried?

Recruiting, nudging, and encouraging contributors is part of an editor's task. Few of us think our own lives are interesting enough to write about. We have gone over them again and again so many times in our own minds, they hardly seem exceptional, particularly to someone else. Every story, every turning point, every woman in this book is exceptional.

Overview of the Contents

True to Ourselves

The first section, "True to Ourselves," begins with the story of explorer Ann Bancroft, the first woman ever to reach the North Pole on skis. Months of harsh and brutal training, necessary for survival in the frozen wilderness, did not prepare her for her new role as pioneering first woman or for the resistance that her dream of leading the first all-woman expedition to the South Pole would engender.

Ellen Hume, executive director of PBS's Democracy Project, writes about the practice of ethical journalism. By trial and error she learned the value of trusting her own instincts and bearing witness to the truth.

Ruth J. Simmons, the president of Smith College, recalls the lessons of a wise and inspiring teacher. Simmons, who grew up in segregated Texas in the 1940s and 1950s, gives a profoundly moving account of how she learned the principles of self-worth, the dignity of work, and enduring grace from her mother.

Mary Dent Crisp, founder of the Republican Coalition for Choice and former co-chair of the Republican National Committee, writes about her evolution to feminism as she faced personal and professional crises that challenged her principles and changed her life.

Woman Power

Rosalie E. Wahl was the first woman appointed to the Minnesota Supreme Court. Her readiness for a public role and the resurgent women's movement converged in the 1970s. Wahl brings to life the joys, pressures, and responsibilities that come with the position of being first. She cautions us to remember that no woman arrives at a place all on her own.

Bella S. Abzug, feminist and former member of Congress, fulfilled her lifetime commitment to women's equality and full political participation. Her essay, which she wrote just weeks before her death, is a call to action and testimony to the struggles of others to make possible the achievements of those women who followed.

The life of U.S. Senator Olympia J. Snowe was altered forever when her mother died of breast cancer. Her advocacy for changing public policy on issues related to women's health is in large measure a commitment to ensure that fewer children experience the premature loss of a mother.

Carmen Delgado Votaw, public policy director for United Way of America, takes us back to the day in 1978 when Bella Abzug was fired as co-chair of President Carter's National Advisory Committee for Women. Votaw, the other co-chair, had to make a critical choice that meant risking her future opportunities for advancement in politics. With this book comes a twentieth reunion of sorts. In addition to Carmen Votaw and Bella Abzug, Mary Crisp and I served on the National Advisory Committee for Women. Votaw's story is our story too.

Representative Eva M. Clayton of North Carolina wanted to be a medical missionary as a child. Instead, as she explains in her essay, community service and politics became the vehicles for implementing her mission to help the disadvantaged, especially the rural poor.

The Measure of Woman

In "The Measure of Woman" we learn about the commitment of four women to something larger than themselves. Kathleen Kennedy Townsend, lieutenant governor of Maryland, begins by defining the measure of a woman as the extent to which her priorities involve values that transcend materialism and individualism. She calls for a renewed commitment by women and men in behalf of principles and causes that are worth fighting for.

Carol Moseley-Braun is the first African American woman ever elected to the U.S. Senate. She describes her arrival in the Senate and celebrates the efforts of her forbears who made that moment possible. Moseley-Braun calls on all Americans to work toward the elimination of artificial barriers to equality and justice.

Sarah Brady, the chair of Handgun Control, exemplifies a commitment to service in behalf of a cause worth fighting for. She explains what made her an activist. Although her interest in politics began at a young age, she was thrust into a public role she never anticipated.

Barbara Roberts, the first woman governor of Oregon, became a citizen lobbyist as a mother determined to protect her son at all costs. Without money or powerful connections, she worked her way from the grass roots to the highest political office in her state.

Turning Points

In "Turning Points," the authors write about events that changed the direction of their lives, challenged their integrity, or shaped their values and purpose.

Christine Todd Whitman, the governor of New Jersey, tells how she confronted the lie, betrayal, and boast of a key strategist in her first gubernatorial campaign.

Representative Patsy T. Mink trained to become a doctor, and like other women in *True to Ourselves,* ran head-on into discrimination. She writes about the turning point in her life that made her a leader in American politics.

Tipper Gore, the second lady of the United States, reveals how her mother's secret led to her advocacy on behalf of the mentally ill. Her husband's decision to run for Congress was a turning point for Gore, who had begun a career as a photographer.

Polly B. Baca, former Colorado state senator, is the first Hispanic woman ever to serve in the leadership of a state senate. She takes us on her public and private journey, candidly sharing her life's lessons and the stressful existence of a politician, activist, and single mother.

New Directions

In "New Directions," the final part of the book, five writers present ideas for the reader to consider as we head into a new millennium, century, and decade.

Political strategist and pollster Celinda C. Lake tells us about her first encounters with sex discrimination. She explores her findings about the gender gap and discusses its future influence on American political campaigns and the outcome of elections.

Angela E. Oh, an attorney and member of President Clinton's Initiative on Race, discusses the reality of America's multicultural future and the need to move beyond narrow definitions of race and racism.

CNN correspondent and author Maria Hinojosa tells us why she long considered herself an "other" growing up in America. Now her "otherness" is something she celebrates, and it informs her reporting as she gives voice to society's voiceless. She chose to be interviewed for her chapter, which also includes a description of her work as a volunteer artist in New York City.

Amy R. Simon is a pollster, feminist, and activist. When her mother died, Simon committed herself to social change. She writes about implementing her goal, beginning in high school. Simon gives an insider's perspective on the stresses and joys of young people who work in presidential campaigns and how she helped organize a young women's political network in Washington, D.C.

Federal judge Vicki Miles-LaGrange discloses the pain of a personal encounter with the evils of racism and the parental guidance that shaped her character. She writes a plea for diversity, not as a shallow cliche, but as a genuine commitment to implementing the greatness of America's promise.

Acknowledgments

The League of Women Voters is very grateful to the contributors for their provocative essays and the time and energy they devoted to making this book possible.

My deep appreciation goes to President Becky Cain and the national board of the League of Women Voters for the confidence they gave me to implement my vision of a book that would embody the League's mission.

I owe immense thanks to Monica Sullivan, the director of publishing, and her former assistant Andrea Sharples in the League's national office for their patience, support, and advice. I am especially grateful to Alan Shrader, my editor at Jossey-Bass, for his wise counsel and trust.

Lewisburg, Pennsylvania   Nancy M. Neuman
June 1998

TRUE TO OURSELVES

To my husband, Mark,
and our children, Deborah,
Jennifer, and Jeffrey, with love

—*N.M.N.*

TRUE TO OURSELVES

ANN BANCROFT is the first woman to travel across the ice to both the North and South Poles. She traveled by dogsled to the North Pole as the only female member of the 1986 Steger International Polar Expedition. She was team leader for the American Women's Expedition, a group of four women who skied more than 660 miles to reach the South Pole in 1993. A former physical education and special education teacher in Minneapolis schools, she is an instructor for Wilderness Inquiry, which helps disabled and able-bodied individuals enjoy wilderness experiences. She has received numerous awards, including induction into the Women's Hall of Fame in 1995 and MS. Woman of the Year in 1987. She holds a B.S. degree from the University of Oregon and an honorary degree from Northland College.

Being Clear in Passion and Desire

ANN BANCROFT

JOINING A TEAM of seven men and forty-nine male dogs to travel to the North Pole in 1986 was a childhood dream come true (at least the part about traveling in the Arctic by dog team, but I was willing to sift through pieces of the equation to get to that dream). I had no idea that this experience would change not only my life but, more important, how I perceived what I could do with my life.

I quit my job as a gym and special education teacher at a small elementary school in South Minneapolis. After packing all my winter clothing and equipment and a tent, I moved in October 1985 to live and train with the rest of the team in the northern woods of Minnesota. In mid-winter we left my home state to do the last two months of training on Baffin Island in northeast Canada.

From Baffin Island, we would continue north in our travels to arrive at the jumping-off spot for the expedition itself, the northern tip of Canada that meets the Arctic Ocean. From this place, we would embark on our two-month journey to the top of the world.

The isolation of our eight months of training had negative and positive aspects. The drawback was loneliness from being so far away from family and friends, amplified because I was the only woman on the team. In looking back, I realize that the advantage was being hidden from the news media in hard-to-find wilderness camps as we prepared for our journey. I had only hints of the public pressure that was building in the event that I made history as the first woman to reach the top of the world across the ice.

On balance, I considered the isolation to be positive, because I felt a great deal of pressure, both self-imposed and underlying within the group. I needed to do this trip for me, first and foremost, and staying focused on the goal was essential to stay safe. Trusting your instincts and knowing yourself and how you respond in certain situations is critical for survival in harsh, remote environments. Listening to outside voices, no matter how well meaning, can be life-threatening.

Going to the North Pole by dog team was the heart of the dream for me. Being the first woman to do so would be an added bonus but not the driving force to my desire. At the time I was very naive not only about the media and how coverage can shape an event but also about the pressures created with that coverage. I was relieved to be so far away.

Deep within I understood that I simply had to go forth and do what I knew how to do: push and pull sleds on the Arctic Ocean and live out my dream. The isolation helped keep me on course with what I believed in my core but struggled to articulate. Without that distance from "normal" life, I might have gotten caught up in all the agendas of others and have lost my way.

Inch by Inch

Once we started on the expedition, our days were filled with long hours spent pushing sleds that were much too heavy for dogs and people. Bitter cold temperatures of seventy-five degrees below zero Fahrenheit enshrouded our dimly lit days in the early weeks of March. As expected, the frozen ocean was very rough. Huge walls of ice buckled up to form what we called mountain ranges but are known as pressure ridges. Some were thirty feet tall and demanded that we go ahead of the sleds to chip and cut a path or road to get the sleds up and over these impasses. All of this made our progress very slow in terms of miles and our work each day and night very long indeed.

Our group's hope for the expedition was to share the experience and feelings of those early explorers to the North Pole. In order to gain a glimpse into their world, we would not ask for any food drops along the way. Although we carried a radio, its purpose was for emergency use only; it would not be used to receive any other outside assistance, including messages from home. Yet even with these guidelines in place in our frozen world, the outside did penetrate.

After twenty-five days of struggle, as we inched our way closer to our destination, one of the physically largest members of our group cracked his ribs and opted to be air-lifted out. The realities of society invaded my world. The curiosity about who was requesting an evacuation brought inquiries about whether the smallest in the group, "the woman," was coming out.

When a plane with skis landed on the ice, two reporters and two cameramen moved around our camp snapping pictures and interviewing each one of us. That I was not the one with the taped midsection astonished them. Their surprise was revealed by the tone of their questions as they asked me what life had been like so far on this journey. They were also caught off-guard by my upbeat demeanor. In all of that cold, gray, basic existence, I was having fun. They were not only surprised but confused.

The media left as quickly as they came, and we were sealed up again within our own reality. The outside world, with all its attitudes and happenings, became very distant and less important. In that hour-long visit, I got a clear sense once again that my making it to the pole was not just important to me but to others as well, particularly women.

That thought frightened me. There was much ahead, and although there were moments of fun, this was clearly the hardest task I had ever undertaken. I wanted to stand at the top of the world for myself, my family, my friends who had helped me get this far, and, now, for others, most of whom I did not know. After that plane flew away, I pushed the sleds with a fuller purpose. I believed then that a shift in my thinking had taken place. In retrospect, however, I realize that a clarity of attitude was beginning to emerge.

On May 2, 1986, six of us reached the North Pole. We became the first explorers to reach the pole without aerial logistics since Robert E. Peary in 1909. I returned from the North Pole on May 4, 1986. My world was turned upside down. Previously a total unknown, having been simply the low totem on the pole, I was suddenly elevated to a status very close to the leaders.

The First Woman

I began traveling around the country giving interviews and lectures—all because I was the first known woman to travel across the ice to the North Pole. Over time, I realized I had always wanted to achieve a "first" as part of my childhood dream. Fear of failure had pushed thoughts of fulfillment far away from my conscious thought, even though many people expressed their hopes for me to achieve this goal. Words such as "role model" or "heroine" made me want to disappear. My fear of disappointing others conveniently pushed this element of the dream aside.

Not until I was addressing a group of students did I finally understand that I had already been a role model as a teacher and coach long before going to the Pole. As the pieces started to fall into place, the burden I once felt began to lighten. I began to embrace the entire dream I had at the age of fourteen. My sense of purpose was returning, and where once there had been a weight, now there was energy.

I began to set my sights on a new journey with a renewed sense of purpose. As before, I returned to the dreams of my childhood: to lead an all-women's team to Antarctica and make history at the bottom of the world. This expedition would share some similarities with the North Pole project, but much would be different.

A New Classroom

Once again I understood the importance of being clear in passion and desire. I knew that success could safely be achieved only if you first have a basic love of the activity and a raw curiosity of place. Being a few years older and having shared many stories with women around the country, I appreciated much more clearly all that I wanted to achieve on Antarctica. I now understood that my passion would drive me and that it was no longer just simply about reaching a distant destination.

In the desire to travel in wild places simply, in realms untouched by humans, other agendas can still lurk within. The fear of disappointing other people that had haunted me as I labored to the North Pole had obscured a very important element of my youthful dream. In my life and work, I wanted to make a difference.

As I planned and prepared for the rigors of Antarctica, I realized that this undertaking was part of my vocation and that the Poles were my new classroom for teaching. I was blending both my passions—my passion for children and my passion for the wilderness. I hoped that my lessons would help break down the barriers that exist for women and girls.

I had learned on the Arctic Ocean that people's attitudes can be far more formidable than the huge walls of ice we had to overcome. I also realized that I was capable of achieving a great deal by simply stepping forward and being true to myself, even when failure was a possibility.

My three female teammates and I encountered many barriers long before we reached Antarctica. Because we did not plan to include men or dogs on this expedition, we had difficulty finding anyone who would believe that we could or should attempt to pull

240-pound sleds in the harshest environment of the globe. When we finally did find people who believed in us, they were mainly schoolchildren and women.

Media attention was sparse and sponsorship nonexistent. We all have moments when we are required to reach deep within ourselves—for instance, when confronting a driving headwind or skiing in a suffocating blizzard. I had confidence that my passion would carry me on the ice of Antarctica during very difficult times, but in the four years of preparation, while we gathered the necessary support for the Antarctica expedition, I had to call upon my passion to energize me even more than was necessary on the trip itself.

With the help of teachers around the country, we developed a curriculum around the expedition and Antarctica that got both teachers and students excited about the journey. The curriculum included math, science, geography, and women's issues. Our mileage and navigation were incorporated into math lessons at various levels.

The lack of sponsorship to support our journey developed classroom discussions about attitudes and how women are perceived in the media and advertising. Each training trip that we took to Canada or Greenland gave us the opportunity to talk to students about preparation (homework), environments, and cultures. We included in our teaching the small failures and successes we had along the way in learning to work and live as a team. All this and much more were put into motion before the expedition left Minnesota in October 1992, bound for icy Antarctica.

A Dream Team

When we arrived on Antarctica, the pilots who deposited us at the edge of the continent invoked one last time the spirit of the obstacles we had encountered during the previous four years of preparation. The pilots thought we were too small physically to do the task, and since they had never seen women before in this frozen land, they were convinced they would be called in to evacuate us.

Women's presence on Antarctica, although growing, is still small, and skepticism remains large. The attitudes of the pilots only fueled the flames of an inner fire in me during those first few cold days as we leaned over our ski tips to begin pulling the sleds that were double our body weight. But in remote excursions, one quickly becomes enshrouded in the isolation and the day-to-day survival. The desire to prove the pilots and any other disbelievers wrong was erased by the Antarctic winds and replaced by the steady rhythm of our bodies, which strengthened as they became a part of that huge sled that constantly shadowed each of us.

Unlike my North Pole experience, I didn't need to discover through the journey that there were many layers to the dream. I was now not only comfortable with being called a role model, I understood that by following my heart I could inspire others to chase their dreams and aspirations.

Although the fear of failure and possible disappointment of others still followed me onto the ice, it would no longer let me deny all that I wanted to do and change. Instead, I would learn another lesson: I was not instigating change alone.

All the people who supported us and believed in us, as women with all that we could accomplish, were agents of change. I gained a fuller knowledge of the power of coming together—that in coming together, collectively we can make a difference. As I stood at the bottom of the world with my three team members on January 14, 1993, I had the overwhelming feeling of standing with all who believed in us and our dream.

ELLEN HUME is the executive director of the Democracy Project at the Public Broadcasting Service (PBS). With more than twenty-five years of experience reporting and commenting on national politics for newspapers and television, she is the author of the prize-winning study *Tabloids, Talk Radio, and the Future of News.* She formerly appeared on *Reliable Sources* (CNN) and *Washington Week in Review* (PBS). From 1983 to 1988 she was a political correspondent for the *Wall Street Journal* and from 1977 to 1983 was a Washington-based reporter for the *Los Angeles Times.* She was executive director and senior fellow at Harvard University's Joan Shorenstein Barone Center on the Press, Politics, and Public Policy and a lecturer at the Kennedy School of Government from 1988 to 1993. She is a graduate of Radcliffe College.

Capturing Opportunities for Leadership

ELLEN HUME

I DECIDED AT AGE TEN that I wanted to be a newspaper reporter, for reasons both sacred and profane. First, the silliest reason: in the popular culture there were very few female role models that crossed my radar. As it happened, two of the most interesting ones were newspaper reporters: Superman's girlfriend Lois Lane and comic strip heroine Brenda Starr (the only other redhead I knew about who amounted to anything). It looked like enormous fun, solving mysteries, having terrific adventures with handsome do-gooder guys, and finding out how things *really* worked.

But what sealed the deal was much more serious. I read *The Diary of Anne Frank* and at the same time learned about Quaker and other religious teachings to bear witness to the world. These powerful influences came together, convincing me that if we were more vigilant and vocal, evils like the Holocaust might be prevented next time. We could at least ensure that never again could people say they "didn't know" what was happening to their neighbors.

So the hope was that I, as a reporter, could make a positive difference. If one were in the right place at the right time, one could help expose crooks and honor unsung heroes. One could be the eyes and ears of the "little guy," helping empower people with information they otherwise wouldn't know.

I knew that in order to do the job well, I would have to give up certain things. We would strive to be "objective," abandoning any right to advocate a particular set of ideas or policy approaches as we covered an issue. We would try to give everyone a fair hearing, and leave it to the public and the politicians to follow up on the facts that we had gathered. That was how democracy was supposed to work.

My ideals collided immediately with harsh realities. As I searched for my first job, it seemed that the world didn't want to be saved—at least not by me. The man at Associated Press had a job opening, but he took one look at me and said, "Forget it." He couldn't hire a woman. "You'll be attacked on the streets of Boston," he said, adding that I also would be scooped by our chief rivals at United Press International at some point because I'd get a flat tire on the way to a story and not know how to change it.

Fortunately I didn't give up. I found myself a reporting job nine months later at the weekly *Somerville Journal,* which launched my journalism career. I learned how to change a tire and studied karate. I resolved to go back and break that AP man's desk in two after I changed his tires, but he retired before I got the chance.

How Things Really Worked

It is hard to remember now, as women openly exercise their influence all across America, how circumscribed most of us were as we came of age thirty years ago. We had been told by our Harvard professors that we were the future leaders of the world. But when we graduated in 1968, it became clear that they were talking only to the men. Discrimination on the basis of race and sex was the norm in virtually every institution.

The women's movement had not yet awakened us to our own potential. A young black leader fighting for racial justice said derisively that the best position for women in the civil rights movement was "prone." The phrases "affirmative action" and "sexual harassment" were not in our vocabularies. It was almost impossible to be taken seriously, whether you were a traditional mother, a would-be career woman, or—horrors!—combining the two.

It's not surprising, then, that many of us were crippled by self-doubt. We thought women would never be able to win Rhodes scholarships, become partners at big law firms, or even get their own credit cards and mortgages.

We were supposed to be the loyal shadows to the men in power. We didn't dare to hope that they would change the baby's diapers, but we did wish they would let us finish our sentences. There was a sort of grim humor about it all, as actress Lee Grant illustrated when she observed in the 1970s that she'd been "married to one Fascist and one Marxist and neither one would take the garbage out."

It might have been easy to conclude that politics was irrelevant to us, since the power belonged to the men. It was tempting to believe that nothing would ever change for the better anyway, so why bother to try? But fortunately, some women and men didn't accept that idea.

These women and men led the legal and political battles that enlarged our civil rights laws in the 1960s and 1970s. The public arena began to offer women and minorities real opportunities for diverse contributions. American culture was changed dramatically because some people took a chance on making a difference. So I came to understand, firsthand, why politics mattered to me and to everyone. Unfortunately, others also taught me how politics can be a force for evil, rather than for progress.

Reporting Reality

As a *Los Angeles Times* reporter in the 1970s, I found myself covering some of the most bizarre political terrorism of our time, including exploits of Sara Jane Moore, who narrowly failed in her assassination attempt against President Gerald Ford, and the Symbionese Liberation Army, a pathetic band of half a dozen middle-class suburban kids who thought that kidnaping newspaper heiress Patty Hearst would set off a revolution in America's black ghettos.

I doubt that more accurate and timely information could have persuaded them to take more reasonable approaches to injustice, for they surely must have been crazy as well as ill-informed. But I felt it was more important than ever to keep bearing witness to realities, in order for democracy to survive the paranoid fanatics. I found myself looking for stories about what works as well as what doesn't in American politics.

It remained very difficult, at times, to be the unbiased witness I was supposed to be. When I flew in the back of a cargo plane to Cambodia on Thanksgiving Day 1979, I was pressured in midair by the relief group sponsoring our flight to write "positive" stories about the relief shipments. Children were starving across Cambodia, they noted, and if I didn't write nice stories about the way the new Cambodian government was handling these emergency supplies, that government would cut off future shipments.

I had committed to being a reporter, not a relief worker, so I told them that I was going to stick with my original job and bear witness to whatever the true story had to be—even if it resulted in a cutoff of aid to the children. Fortunately, the relief shipments worked well, so I never had to follow through on that terrible choice.

When I toured Phnom Penh's Tuol Sleng prison and saw the just-vacated torture chambers, the pits of bones, the killing fields of Pol Pot's regime, which had just been ousted by this new Cambodian government, I learned again the core lesson: politics matters. We need witnesses to be sure everyone understands when things are going wrong, and why.

Everything that I learned in my journalism career was through trial and error, and I was very lucky that my mistakes didn't kill me; they made me stronger. Most of all, I trusted my instincts and protected my integrity. That meant I could sleep most nights, knowing that I was at least trying to do an honest job.

When I started, I had hoped to help citizens discover their own power to influence the events of our time. But too often we journalists ended up chasing the big splashy stories, rather than the ones that would truly make a difference.

Unlikely Sources

In the end the special contributions emerged mostly by accident, in small stories at unexpected moments—like the day I was asked to write a feature story about a woman named Anais Uren, who had learned to paint with her toes after her hands became paralyzed by multiple sclerosis.

When I arrived at her nursing home, I was too late; she had gone blind and could no longer paint even with her toes. She was only fifty-six, and she looked like Ingrid Bergman. I stayed for awhile by her bedside to talk. She couldn't see, her body was paralyzed, and it was hard to understand what she was saying. But she could still hear and feel and think.

She told me her life story, radiating spirit and courage. I went back to my office and wrote: "There are times when all of us have asked ourselves, why do we go on living? No one has asked it more often than Anais Uren." People read about her extraordinary survivor's spirit. They wrote her letters from all over the world. She touched peoples' lives, and they touched hers back.

This, then, was the most important lesson of all, taught to me by a blind and paralyzed woman who was at the end of her life. The opportunities for leadership arrive without warning, and sometimes very close to home.

You can't force your solutions onto an unwilling world, as the terrorists tried to do. You can't solve it all by yourself. But anyone can make a difference if she responds to a genuine opportunity to help. The invitation could come any day, just when you least expect it, from a most unlikely source.

RUTH J. SIMMONS became president of Smith College in
1995. From 1992 to 1995 she was vice provost at Princeton
University, where she had been an administrator from 1983
to 1990. From 1990 to 1992 she was provost at Spelman College. She has been a faculty member at the University of New
Orleans, California State University Northridge, Spelman College, and Princeton University. Her teaching and research interests are primarily in the literature of Francophone Africa
and the Caribbean. She has written on the works of David
Diop and Aime Cesaire and is the author of a book on education in Haiti. In 1996 Simmons was named a CBS Woman of
the Year, an NBC Nightly News Most Inspiring Woman, and
a *Glamour* magazine Woman of the Year. She holds a B.A. degree from Dillard University, a Ph.D. degree from Harvard
University, and numerous honorary degrees.

Recognizing Moments of Learning

RUTH J. SIMMONS

U PON BECOMING A COLLEGE president, I learned that I was thought, by virtue of that position, to possess a reservoir of wisdom, knowledge, and power that seemed, to some, worthy of understanding. The curious and the ambitious found their way to my door to posit questions intended to reveal the secrets of my accomplishments: Was there a particular course of study that was fruitful (surely not the romance languages I studied)? Were there work experiences that I skillfully arranged to build a reservoir of knowledge useful to a college presidency? How did I identify the right professional and educational mentors?

When these questions first came to me, I was at a loss to reply. Like many, I had followed a path not through a system carefully charted but by the fortuitous intrusion of opportunity. Shaped by the social limitations of the pre–civil rights 1940s and 1950s, my preteen and teenage years held little promise of great accomplishment. Most of my eleven sisters and brothers before me had gone into military service or early blue-collar work as soon as their ages allowed; their primary concern was finding a reliable means of supporting themselves as young adults.

My early notions of adulthood presented visions of dignified work in the tradition of my parents and their friends. Those visions were not of lofty accomplishments but of survival in a time of upheaval and challenge.

I am convinced that my parents, too, shared these relatively modest goals for their children. Those who have studied or recall the economic and social cultures of the southern states in the 1940s and 1950s can readily understand this willful suppression of aspiration. On the brink of integration in 1963, when I graduated from high school, schools in Houston were decidedly and committedly segregated. Racially classified, like the neighborhoods (or "wards" as they were known) that they served, these schools furthered the aims of helping one's community and living an honorable life safe from the racism that surrounded us.

If we aspired to be teachers, physicians, ministers, or other professional workers, we imagined carrying out those jobs in the service of our race, since all the teachers, physicians, ministers, and office workers that we knew served their own racial communities. Few of us envisioned journeying beyond our racial context to work in the stern stone buildings that framed the city skyline not far from our modest neighborhoods.

Those able to cross the boundaries of segregated neighborhoods to interact with whites did so primarily in the capacity of subservience; they worked as servers, housekeepers, custodians, and other service workers in neighborhoods where they could not live and in businesses that they often could not frequent. My mother and father both crossed those boundaries, returning home with stories of how the other side lived and behaved, admonishing their children to retain always a sense of themselves and their worth. No doubt, from their own interactions outside the racially homogeneous neighborhood where we lived, they knew we would eventually face bigotry that would undermine our sense of self and community. However, these lessons did not make a firm imprint initially, since we scarcely could imagine the integrated world playing a major role in our lives. For me, it was the daily routine of school that seemed to offer the needed insights into challenges of the adult world.

As a student in high school, I thrived on the opportunities placed before me by teachers who were alert to the need to provide rich educational and cultural experiences for children whose parents did not have the means or time to supplement a school's standard offerings. The school experience, in what seemed to me a limitless expanse of promise and fulfillment, was a magnificent place where people shared my love of books, where there were varied resources to satisfy my intellectual needs, and where teachers served as guides and interpreters for the many worlds I could not experience firsthand.

Finally, here was an environment in which my ardent interest and enthusiasm for learning as well as my ambition and competitiveness found praise and support. I was certain that education held the key to all good things and particularly to any professional success that I could imagine for myself.

A Sudden Loss

My mother died weeks before my sixteenth birthday, leaving me bereft and confused. Without grief counseling, I was left to cope with this remarkable and defining event in my life by throwing myself more deeply into school experiences, which provided not only a refuge but also a vaunted source of inspiration. Yet without a means of understanding how to cope with the sudden loss of a parent, I needed a way to harmonize my love and respect for my mother with my sincere regard for matters academic.

Eventually, alongside the course of study that I followed in high school and college, I began to try systematically to retrieve, understand, and integrate the teachings of my mother. Over time, as her example came into stronger relief, I developed (initially out of grief but eventually out of a deep appreciation of its value) an understanding that what I had learned from this simple yet elegantly informed woman held as much value as all the books I had read, the courses I had taken, the colleges that I had attended, and the degrees that I earned.

In my quest for formal learning, I overlooked for many years the greatest source of inspiration and learning in my life. My mother's achievement was to instill in me the means to live honorably without her; like those of any good teacher, her methods ensured that when I no longer had access to her voice, I would be guided by a treasury of principles and wise examples for the rest of my life.

Fannie Campbell

Fannie Campbell was one of five children born to parents in rural East Texas. Her father died when she was quite young, leaving her mother to rear her children alone. My mother's coming of age amidst the stubbled fields of Daley community in Grapeland, Texas (called Sandy Flats because of the sandy soil of the region), must have been remarkable, for she frequently recounted chilling stories of her family's struggles. Her father had purchased sixty acres of farm land in the area, and upon his death his widow, Emma Campbell, was able to farm the land and thus sustain her family.

Because the children were called upon to work the fields so that produce could be raised for income and subsistence, few of them were able to have a complete education. My mother finished eight years of the most rudimentary education; she knew how to read, write, and do math but had only halting skills in all.

Her own difficult circumstances had left my mother with one prevailing goal when she married and had her own children: to live long enough to see all her children to adulthood. She almost accomplished that, since her youngest was almost sixteen when she died. Doubtless because of the vicissitudes of her own life, though minimally educated, she sought to arm her children for life by teaching them how to live with dignity and purpose. I credit these teachings with setting me on the course for a presidency.

Particularly acute memories are the moments when my mother invited me to see her work and to understand the commitment she had to the highest quality of effort. As a domestic worker, she performed a variety of housekeeping tasks for other families even while she kept her own household running. She worked as a part-time housekeeper for several families, and on days when she remained at home, she took in ironing.

I recall the many mounds of clothes that families would bring to our house. Occasionally, I would help sprinkle these with water and roll them into bundles to await ironing. My mother would sometimes iron for many hours to finish the loads that had been left. She proceeded in her work with a certain order: the collars of shirts were the first to be tackled, then the rear horizontal cross-section of the shirt, next the tops of the front panels. Next came the sleeves and then the remainder of the shirt. She kept a bowl of water nearby to moisten dry areas or to retouch spots that had been inadequately pressed. As she ironed, she talked to us about life, character, and the challenges that living inexorably presents.

When I accompanied her to the homes she cleaned, it was more to keep her company and to be instructed than to provide useful help, because I was too inexperienced to be of great assistance. She was exceptionally thorough in her work. Often she worked a "half day," which was of course less expensive for the employer and more difficult for her, since employers generally expected a full day's work for the halved wage. Yet she went about this work without any audible complaint, intent always on accomplishing well what she set out to do.

I think that I must have been puzzled that my mother showed neither evidence of resentment of the kind of work she did nor scorn for the people who exploited her diligence. I have since known many laborers and domestic workers, and among them, scorn for their employers is a common sentiment. By nature a subdued person, my mother carried herself as if she were someone to be reckoned with. No, she was not the overbearing stereotype of the black maid one sees in film, but her bearing and physiognomy were such that even those who refused her the proper salutation as a married woman were moved to accord her the proper deference. She was herself deferential to her employers without being obsequious; her glance bore a kind of warning that disrespect would not be tolerated. (That glance, when leveled at her children in public, signaled that all mischief should cease.)

Yet for all the strength she exemplified, my mother did not seem to think of herself as a powerful or even important person. That she was an important person became singularly evident to me as I grew into adulthood and began to understand better the rarity of the attributes that she possessed. I grew to realize that it was her example that had propelled me toward achievement. Finally, the different spheres of my life were becoming reconciled.

A Wise and Inspiring Teacher

Fannie Campbell is by far the greatest influence of my life and the person to whom I am most indebted for what I have achieved of any consequence. A wise and inspiring teacher, she taught me to value no person merely on the basis of his or her material worth. Handing down to me stories of courage in the face of bigotry, she suggested a way for me to survive the rigors of intolerance in American society.

From how she could with grace, magnanimity, and aplomb carry out the most unfulfilling work, I learned not to accord esteem on the basis of the kind of work one is consigned to perform. Carrying herself with quiet poise, she instructed me in how to assert my views firmly but without swagger and clamor. Finally, in the world I inhabit—a world of cultural, social, and intellectual elites—people are most often prized for what they have accumulated or for achievements that have been widely noted and rewarded. Value is too often confused with intellectual miserliness, affluence, and social prominence.

My mother, Fannie Campbell, taught me that the most accomplished and worthy people we encounter in life may be clad in the wrong clothes and speak in broken language. She taught me the privilege of labor and instilled in me the will to work unstintingly in all that I attempt. Many of the most accomplished men and women have been shaped by uneducated women who used their native intelligence and humanity to instruct us all in how to live lives of meaning, sacrifice, and accomplishment.

So when I am asked how I accomplished all that I have, I inevitably and most gratefully point to the lessons learned from the example and teachings of a maid who tried to teach me to be a person of worth. As president of Smith College, a place of uncommon resources, I urge students to remember that they will benefit from those resources but that they will perhaps learn more from unexpected sources. I admonish them to be watchful and open-minded lest they fail to recognize those moments of learning.

MARY DENT CRISP is founder and former chair of the Republican Coalition for Choice and was co-chair of the Republican National Committee from 1977 to 1980. She chaired John Anderson's presidential campaign in the fall of 1980 after warning the Republican National Convention that its platform reversal on the proposed Equal Rights Amendment and its endorsement of a constitutional amendment to ban abortion would undermine the party's ability to gain majority status. From 1984 to 1990 she was senior adviser and political director to Business Executives for National Security. She is a graduate of Oberlin College and holds honorary degrees from Oberlin and Cedar Crest Colleges.

My Journey to Feminism

MARY DENT CRISP

W HAT MATTERS MOST to me today is also what is best for this nation. I did not always feel this way. When I was thirty-seven years old, I chose to serve my country by becoming deeply involved in the Republican Party, with the hope of making a difference and creating a better world. Ultimately, Republican politics served as the framework for much larger issues—my evolution as an individual and my dedication to women's equality.

In 1960, I read the *Capitalist Manifesto* by Drs. Adler and Kelso. The book had an enormous impact on me. The essence of the book was that if you want to make a difference in your own life and the life of your community, get involved in politics because it affects every aspect of your life from the cradle to the grave. In addition, my experience at Oberlin College enabled me to realize that the world could be a better place and that I had a responsibility to help make it so.

In 1961, as a young housewife living in Arizona, my role was clearly defined, as it was for many women of my generation—wife, mother, and volunteer. I took my first step into the political world as a Goldwater Republican by walking into a GOP headquarters and volunteering. If anyone had told me then that one day I would hold the number two position in the national Republican Party, my response would have been, "Absolute madness!"

Over many years I worked my way through the ranks of the party organization, from block worker to state vice chair. In 1972, I felt honored when I was elected Arizona's Republican national committeewoman. I was also elected delegate to the 1972 Republican National Convention and served on the platform committee. I remember this experience vividly because it was my first introduction to the Equal Rights Amendment (ERA). Young, intelligent feminists lobbied me to include an ERA plank in the platform. It seemed simply a matter of equal rights, but their sincere passion and commitment to this issue moved me on a deeper level, so I voted yes. Little did I know that many of these women would resurface later in my life as powerful leaders in the fight for women's equality.

My political journey must be seen not only in the context of the Republican Party but also in the context of the women's movement. The Equal Rights Amendment passed Congress in 1972 and moved on to the states for ratification. The Supreme Court's landmark decision *Roe v. Wade* legalizing abortion followed in 1973. I did not consider myself a feminist. I was an active party worker who felt a sense of pride and dignity to be working for a party that had championed justice, equality, and personal freedom.

Being a party activist was educational and gratifying and held great moral value. It gave me a deep feeling of self-dignity, a sense of my fellow human beings, my neighborhood, my community, and my world. It literally transformed my life. The party I served during the 1960s and 1970s was the party of Abraham Lincoln. During that time, the Republican Party was a strong advocate of women's rights, and in 1940, was the first party to include the ERA in its platform.

The Birth of a Feminist

In January 1973, President Nixon was in the White House, Senator Bob Dole was the Republican National Committee chairman, and Anne Armstrong was the co-chair. Under their leadership, the national party launched a nationwide campaign to ratify the Equal Rights Amendment. As Arizona's national committeewoman, I was charged with testifying before the Arizona state legislature on behalf of the ERA.

This experience was extremely shocking because my testimony was not embraced as I had assumed it would be. It was shot down by my own Republican legislators. To add to my amazement, Phyllis Schlafly, a right-wing Republican from the Midwest, was there with her entourage to testify against the ERA.

It was as if a thunderbolt had hit me. I suddenly realized that the ERA was a very significant subject, and it was critical for me to become knowledgeable about all the far-reaching consequences that surrounded it. For the first time, I was aware that the issue of equal rights was a growing source of contention within the GOP. It was unsettling to observe this developing chasm around one of the fundamental principles of the party.

By 1974, Watergate's dark shadow was upon the nation, and the national committee's position was to defend President Nixon. As evidence mounted against the president, it became increasingly difficult to speak with honesty about party leadership, and I called into question my ability to defend party values.

In early August of the same year, I went on a hiking trip in the Montana wilderness with my family. We were out of touch for ten days, and upon our return we were greeted with the devastating news that President Nixon had left office in disgrace and that Vice President Ford had been sworn in as president of the United States. As the November elections came and went, the Republican Party suffered great losses due to Watergate, and the radical right had made substantial moves within the party against women's rights.

At the 1976 GOP national convention in Kansas City, the internal party struggle was raging. Candidate hopeful Ronald Reagan challenged President Ford for the nomination, further dividing the party on the issue of equality. As secretary of the convention, I was in the thick of things. It was a Ford convention and I was an adamant supporter. The Ford momentum prevailed, defeating Reagan's bid for the nomination.

Immediately following the convention, I was elected secretary of the Republican National Committee (RNC). The November election that followed, in which President Ford lost to Jimmy Carter, was a great disappointment. The RNC members met with President Ford for the last time at the White House in December to bid our farewells. I felt overwhelmed with sadness.

President and Mrs. Ford had carried on the party's ERA legacy during their administration. With their departure, I questioned its future within the Republican party structure. The struggle for party control by the radical right continued. As a Ford supporter and an advocate of the ERA, I soon became a target for their attacks.

During this time, my personal life was shattered when my marriage of twenty-eight years ended in divorce. I was devastated and found myself facing a very unfamiliar world. For the first time in my life, at the age of fifty-three, I was without emotional and economic security. I was a displaced homemaker in need of a job. I had not worked for pay since I had helped my husband through medical school and his internship, more than twenty-five years ago. I was frightened, and the divorce proceedings magnified this feeling; the Equal Rights Amendment once again became very real for me.

Intellectually, I had understood the theory behind the ERA, but it had never before touched me personally in such a significant way. I had believed that I was safe and secure in my marriage. What I discovered during the ugly struggle for my economic rights in the divorce settlement was that my contribution of twenty-eight years as a homemaker, wife, and mother had no dollar value.

I was stunned and demeaned. I felt that being a wife and a mother was the most important contribution I could make to society and that it held great value. I was confused and questioned my overall worth. Divorce had changed my life. Beyond the pain, it ultimately offered new opportunities for growth and freedom beyond my wildest dreams.

Fortunately, my many years as a political activist and my continued education in a master's degree program in political science paid off in the job market. In January 1977, within two months of being divorced, I was elected co-chair of the Republican National Committee. It was a full-time, paid position that required a move to Washington, D.C. My children were in college, so there was nothing holding me back from taking on this new challenge. I left my Arizona home of over twenty years and assumed a new life in the nation's capital.

My experiences as part of the Republican Party had made me a feminist—a strong advocate of rights for women. During the three and a half years that I held the position of co-chair, I faced as part of the working world the same realities that other women had been facing for years. I traveled the nation for the GOP, helping to build and revitalize the party. I saw inequities in the workplace, educational system, job market, and health care. I saw victims of domestic violence and rape and began to understand their needs. As a single woman, I saw how difficult it was for women in this country.

No longer did I lack the passion for the Equal Rights Amendment that was missing for me in 1972. I was deeply committed to helping women, and through the RNC I developed a women's program that included a series of bipartisan seminars and conferences designed to empower women personally, economically, politically. In addition, the program recruited and supported women, many of whom were Republican. Our efforts were rewarded.

The seven years stipulated for the ratification of the Equal Rights Amendment was due to expire in 1979. I persuaded Bill Brock, chairman of the RNC, to support a three-year extension for ratification. I led the party in this effort as we lobbied the Republican members of Congress, marched in Washington, and spoke out at rallies in support of the ERA. These actions only antagonized the radical right, who referred to me as the "Gloria Steinem of the Republican Party."

The party split over the Equal Rights Amendment was manifested in a right-wing challenge to my reelection. However, the challenge was unsuccessful.

As 1980 approached, it became increasingly clear that the future of the ERA was in jeopardy. I could see problems ahead. As Reagan pushed ahead in the presidential primaries, backed by the political right, sources indicated that the Equal Rights Amendment plank would be removed from the party platform. Conversations with people in positions of power, including Maureen Reagan, an adamant supporter of the Equal Rights Amendment, were futile. Support for the ERA faded in the din of the Reagan battle cry.

Personally, I felt betrayed once again. First, by Nixon, then the divorce, and now by the party's abandonment of women's rights. It seemed ironic that the Republican Party, the party of Abraham Lincoln, for which I had worked for so many years, was drastically changing and turning its back on women.

Another dramatic turning point for me came in 1980. It was the first time that my intense loyalty for my country transcended my loyalty to the Republican Party. America's highest ideals of justice, equality, personal rights, and freedom were like a beacon to me. I could not be silent.

Protecting My Ideals

At the time of the Republican National Convention in Detroit, I felt compelled to denounce publicly the party platform that had reneged on a forty-year commitment to the Equal Rights Amendment. Moreover, the platform called for a constitutional amendment to ban abortion. It also stipulated that individuals who were recommended for judicial appointments should believe in the sanctity of human life and respect traditional family values.

I testified against the platform because I believed it compromised the fundamental principles of individual rights and freedom from government interference in our private lives. I said, "The party was about to bury the rights of one hundred million American women under a heap of platitudes." I also stated that I would never turn my back on my commitment to women's rights. Since that time, my professional energy has been focused on protecting women's freedoms and personal rights.

I left Detroit disheartened by the state of the party and joined forces with Independent presidential candidate John Anderson, as chair of his campaign. I believed in his policies and his strong support for the ERA. I traveled in more than thirty states over a three-month period, speaking on his behalf. I believe that my involvement in John Anderson's campaign was the most honorable action that I have taken in American politics.

The ERA was never ratified. All through the 1980s, I continued to speak out against the radical right and support women's equality. From 1984 to 1990, I served as the national political director for Business Executives for National Security. My involvement in this nonpartisan organization was critical because our country was facing a nuclear threat. To me, the issue of national security superseded all other concerns at the time.

Protecting the Right to Choose

In July 1989, I was shocked and angered by the Supreme Court's decision in *Webster* v. *Reproductive Health Services,* which limited a woman's right to choose. I felt a deep threat to all women. The fear of losing our constitutional right to choose gave birth to the Republican Coalition for Choice. The organization was founded as a network of pro-choice Republican activists, working at the grassroots level to organize the pro-choice Republican majority into positions of political power. As founder of this national organization, I chaired the board of directors for a five-year period, until 1994.

Now, in my seventy-fifth year, I have clarity about my life that only comes with the gift of time. I no longer see myself as a Republican politician but as a participant in a much larger world in which women still struggle for equality at all levels.

My political journey often took me into uncharted waters, where personal values and integrity were my only guides. Commitment and staying power led me beyond the boundaries of party politics and toward a worldview that embraces our highest ideals of peace, justice, and equality for all.

Margaret Sanger, founder of Planned Parenthood, stated that "women must own and control their own bodies if ever they are to call themselves free." True equality for a woman is to have complete freedom with regard to her body. The right to choose is the ultimate personal power that we can possess as women. We are in great danger today of losing that power.

The anti-choice drumbeat is not about protecting the unborn fetus. It is more about some men desperately fighting to maintain control over women. Perhaps one needs to define the word "control." Could it be, in the broadest sense, an issue of fear that exists between human beings? Today we are plagued with the real and dominant force of the radical religious right, which uses talk of "family values" as a smoke screen to control women's reproductive freedom. In this context, one must continue to question the agenda of the Promise Keepers as well.

Complacency is a terrible danger. The greatest threat to equality occurs when individuals choose not to be involved. There are many ways to get involved and express our commitment and beliefs to causes, organizations, and the political process.

Equality and freedom are rooted in the kind of government that we have. The plight of women is still burdensome, and the need is greater than ever for increased involvement. Power still flows through our political system, and we must work within it to make a difference.

We are blessed to live in this great, democratic nation, where individuals are important. We do matter. We have the opportunity, the responsibility, and the power to make a difference. The challenge is ours.

WOMAN POWER

ROSALIE E. WAHL is associate justice of the Minnesota Supreme Court, retired. She was the first woman appointed to the
supreme court, where she served from 1977 until her retirement
in 1994. She chaired the Minnesota Supreme Court Task Force
on Gender Fairness in the Courts and Task Force on Race Bias
in the State Judicial System. She was the first woman chair of
the American Bar Association (ABA) Section of Legal Education
and Admissions to the Bar and is past chair of the section's Accreditation Committee. From 1994 to 1995, she chaired the
Wahl Commission for the ABA, which studied the accreditation
process of American law schools. Wahl was clinical professor of
law at William Mitchell College of Law from 1973 to 1977 and
assistant Minnesota state public defender from 1967 to 1973.
She holds a B.A. degree from the University of Kansas and a
J.D. degree from William Mitchell College of Law.

Getting and Being Ready

ROSALIE E. WAHL

WHEN GOVERNOR RUDY PERPICH announced in June 1977 his intention to appoint me to the Minnesota Supreme Court, the first woman ever to serve on that high court, Koryn Horbal, the Democratic Farmer Labor Party (DFL) chairwoman who had fought hard to further the cause of women in politics and government, shook my hand in congratulation and said simply, "Thanks for being ready." I suddenly realized I had spent my entire life "getting ready" without knowing what I was getting ready for.

I hadn't known what I was getting ready for back in that one-room country school in Birch Creek, District 52, Chautauqua County, Kansas, where the excitement of learning first took hold of me, and the dawning realization of the vast unknown possibilities that lay beyond Greer's Hill on one horizon and Standpipe Hill on the other. Outside of Grandma and Aunt Sara, who raised me—Grandma in the Old Stone House, Aunt Sara coming and going from her work in the outside world—teachers were the most important people in my life. Faye Simpson, Lela McKinney, Margaret Spires, Kenneth Henderson, and in high school, "Mrs. Jones, the Lion-Hearted," gave me knowledge and models of being and dreams.

I hadn't known what I was getting ready for when I graduated from Caney High School in 1942, editor, actor, salutatorian, determined to go to the University of Kansas and become a journalist, even if girls weren't generally encouraged to go to the university at that time. Nor had I known what I was getting ready for when I graduated from the University of Kansas at the end of World War II with a degree in sociology, an idealistic hope for the future of the world through the United Nations, and a deep concern for racial equality and economic and social justice.

Marriage, a move to Minnesota, family, and sixteen years intervened before my journey led me to the study of the law. In the fall of 1962, I became a student at William Mitchell College of Law, one of two women in my law school class. I was thirty-eight years old with four children; a fifth was born my second year in law school. I didn't know what I was getting ready for, but I did know I was getting ready.

I knew from my community activities on behalf of the public good that I was tired of sitting outside of doors while the men on the inside made the decisions that affected all our lives. The law, somehow, seemed to be a key to those doors. I can say now that law is the key, or at least one of them, and it is more fun to be on the inside making the decisions.

I became an appellate advocate in criminal law as a state public defender, arguing more than one hundred felony appeals before the Minnesota Supreme Court. I became a professor at William Mitchell College of Law, teaching and also establishing and directing the law school's criminal clinical program. I worked in the courts with the students, representing indigent misdemeanants and looking at the system from the bottom up.

I became a part of the burgeoning women's movement in the 1970s, including Minnesota Women Lawyers, the DFL Feminist Caucus, Minnesota National Organization for Women (NOW), and Minnesota Women's Political Caucus. Those were heady days when we were saying, "If we can't make policy, we won't make coffee." We women lawyers, in our innocence, supposed that the governor of our state did not appoint women to executive and judicial positions in the government because he did not know who we were and what our talents were. We would make a list for him.

I served on the committee that designed the questionnaire to survey the capabilities and expertise of women lawyers and their willingness to serve in appointive office. In due course, I received my questionnaire. A year passed before I returned it because I could not decide how to answer the question, "Would you be willing to accept an appointment to the bench?"

Ready and Willing

Would I be willing to be a judge? So many of the judges in front of whom I had appeared—all male—seemed to be poured into a rigid, authoritative mold. Could I be a good judge and still be myself? It is very important to me to be who I am. Fortunately, I found some male models who were great judges and very much themselves, so I knew it could be done. It also became clear to me that when we were pushing so hard for the appointment of women, the time had come for women to "put up or shut up."

Yes, I was willing. Yes, many women lawyers were willing. But our willingness alone would have availed us nothing. We could have knocked forever on the Minnesota Supreme Court chambers door except that the women of Minnesota had become politically powerful enough to say to the governor, "Nine-zip won't do it."

Lest we women who have achieved success and distinction in any field of endeavor think we have attained our positions by our own efforts alone, we need to think again. I like to paraphrase South

African feminist Olive Schreiner, who said it best in *Dreams* (published by Little, Brown, 1919): Other women before us have made the track to the water's edge, and on their backs we cross over the river to the promised land of freedom and equality.

We women have learned, by necessity and inspiration, to take the brunt of the wind on our wings and lead the flock for a time, one after another. By watching each other meet challenges, we have learned to do things we never thought we could do. Women we admire and learn from show us what is possible. Together we have learned to cross the lines that others—cultural, institutional, masculine others—have drawn for us, so that we may share in the exercise of power and the making of decisions that affect us all.

On June 3, 1977, Governor Rudy Perpich announced his intention to appoint me to serve on the Minnesota Supreme Court. Secretary of State Joan Growe conveyed the announcement that night to a great crowd of four thousand cheering women at the Minnesota Women's Meeting in St. Cloud. In response, I said, in part, "Every person—poor or rich, black or red or brown or white, male or female—has the right to equal justice under law. I will endeavor with the other members of the court to make this dream a reality."

On October 3, 1977, Governor Perpich presented me to the Minnesota Supreme Court as his appointment, and Chief Justice Robert Sheran administered the oath of office. In my remarks I said that the rope that rings the bell of justice must be long enough for even a child to reach, and I promised the governor and the people of the state that I would hear that bell when it rang. I spent the next seventeen years doing my best.

A World of Men

On that October day, I moved into a world of men—good men, learned men, men exercising power to make law and do justice in the State of Minnesota in an exciting and exacting institution, a collegial high court. My colleagues respected me, my seat on the court, and my vote. They were kind, courteous, and helpful, and shared a great sense of humor, but they never let me forget that I was number nine and always the last to speak at conference, except for the chief justice. Often nothing much remained to be said after the others had had their say, but they still listened—and I, too, listened, learned, and did my work, and I made some difference on some cases that year.

One year later I was running statewide to retain that seat on the court, with two sitting district court judges and a former state attorney general hard on my heels. All up and down the state I went, speaking to lawyers everywhere, people in general, and women in particular. Our best piece of campaign literature was a picture of our Minnesota Supreme Court—eight men and one woman. It was worth ten thousand words.

Women across the state closed ranks. They knew that if a woman could not be elected statewide, a governor would never again throw away an appointment by appointing a woman. Justice C. Donald Peterson and I ran a joint campaign—bless his memory—and we didn't spend any money that we did not have. My volunteer committee raised $29,000, mostly at $10-per-person fund-raisers catered by the Women's Political Caucus.

It was a stirring race, even if it was a second full-time job for me because the work of the court still went on. When the votes were in, I had defeated my general election opponent 57 percent to 43 percent. In two subsequent elections, six and twelve years later, I strolled rather than ran because I was unopposed.

The work on the court, demanding but exciting, was the hardest work I have ever done. I quickly realized the power of the office. The writing of opinions that became law was an awful power, one that I tried to use wisely without succumbing to the "black robe disease" of becoming arbitrary and capricious.

In retrospect, I think that initially I did not make the same full use of the power of position (but I learned). I have thought about this since hearing the term used by management expert Rosabeth Moss Kanter in 1996 when she spoke to the International Women's

Forum in Boston. According to my notes, Kanter says that the power of position is the first of the five powers women have. It means using resources at one's command to influence beyond that position—through appointments to committees, setting of agendas, outreach.

A Commitment to Diversity and Equality

The state supreme court is responsible for administration of the state judicial system. In that capacity I helped initiate and chaired both the Supreme Court Task Force on Gender Fairness in the Courts and the Supreme Court Task Force on Race Bias in the State Judicial System. These were enormous undertakings. They involved getting diverse committees of people, both inside and outside the system, to work together and with the public to examine the judicial system from within for evidence of gender and racial bias.

We found evidence—heart-wrenching, conscience-disturbing evidence. We made significant reports to the court and to the state legislature that have led to many changes, both judicial and legislative, with ongoing implementation. These beginnings and this work were major accomplishments of the court during my service there.

We citizens of the United States are a diverse people, and we must bring that diversity into our mostly white criminal justice system and into our mostly white judicial system. We must have diversity in police departments, on corrections and court services staffs, in prosecution and defender offices, in the judiciary, on the bench, and in the courthouses across the state. This means men and women, and it means women and men from both minority and nonminority populations in our communities, from the rank and file to the top levels of administration.

We must do this because, in addition to our knowledge and expertise, we bring who we are along with us when we enter law enforcement or any other part of the criminal justice or judicial system. We bring our backgrounds and experience, our various understandings of cultures and subcultures, of human relations—without which we cannot do the job we must do.

We need intelligent, humane women and men of all colors and backgrounds to grapple with the sexism and racism that are so much a part of our lives and our institutions that we don't even see them. It takes all of us, men and women together, to keep the balance true, the system just, and the public safe.

To my work as liaison between the court and the State Board of Law Examiners, I carried my dual concerns for diversity and equal access to the profession and a high-quality legal education for every lawyer. Those same concerns also sparked ten years of involvement with the Section of Legal Education and Admissions to the Bar of the American Bar Association. I served as the first woman chair of the section, which is the nationally recognized accrediting body for American law schools.

My experience has been that the presence of even one woman on a court, one person of color, one differently abled person, heightens awareness, broadens perspective, and begins to change the court's direction in some way. Gender, my experience of growing up female in this society, enlightened my work on the court. It also enlightened my colleagues, who had only their experience of growing up male, and helped us together to make better, more just decisions. It sometimes took years—as in coming to realize the permanently diminished earning capacity of long-time homemakers cast adrift in midlife, or the harm done to children by sexual abuse.

Doing Justice

Looking back over my opinions, dissents, and special concurrences that address issues of special concern to women, I find that the conflicts sometimes arose over the interpretation of statutes enacted to reform the law and improve the condition of women and children and sometimes over the admissibility of evidence in criminal cases. Sometimes the cause was a matter as simple as a change of name.

In 1981, our court specifically approved the admissibility of evidence of the battered child syndrome in a criminal prosecution. In 1982, however, the court rejected evidence of the rape trauma syndrome in *State v. Saldana*. It held that in a first-degree criminal sexual conduct prosecution wherein the defendant claimed consent, admission of expert testimony concerning typical post-rape symptoms and behavior of rape victims, and the expert's opinion that the complaining witness was a victim of rape and had not fantasized the rape, was reversible error.

I was unable to take part in consideration of this case because I had represented Saldana in another matter as a state public defender. I could, and did, dissent, however, in *State v. McGee* (324 N.W. 2d 234), reversed the same day on the basis of *Saldana*.

I defined the rape trauma syndrome and set out some of the substantial database that supports its existence and reliability. I recognized the qualifications of the state's expert witness, Dr. Springrose, as an authority with specific experience concerning psychological aftershock commonly experienced by rape victims, known as rape trauma syndrome. I argued, "Dr. Springrose did not testify, as did the expert witness in Saldana, as to whether, in his opinion, the rape actually occurred. Rather, he discussed some of the complainant's psychological symptoms after the alleged rape and stated that he found these symptoms to be consistent with rape trauma syndrome. Such evidence is probative on the issue of consent and thus helpful to the jury in resolving the conflicting facts of this case concerning that issue." Justice C. Donald Peterson joined the dissent.

Saldana and *McGee* were decided August 31, 1982. The next day, on September 1, 1982, five years after I joined the court, M. Jeanne Coyne, appointed by Governor Al Quie, became our second woman justice. It took me four months to realize, with a sudden rush of discovery, that no longer did I have to be all the things a woman on the court should be—Justice Coyne could be some of them. That numbers make a difference became more perceptible with the appointment of each new woman justice—Esther Tomljanovich in 1990, Sandra Gardebring in 1991. Each of us, in her own way, could increasingly use that very considerable elbow room the court provides.

When *New York Times* reporter David Margolick wandered out to Minnesota to see for himself, he wrote in "Women's Milestone: Majority on the Minnesota Court," on February 22, 1991, that though women were entering the legal profession in record numbers, "no powerful legal institution . . . has ever been dominated by women, until now."

Margolick found that my appointment had been "more prelude than token" and concluded that while "no one is predicting that the new female majority on the seven-member Minnesota Court will instantly produce changes in its jurisprudence," some lawyers were predicting heightened sensitivity to cases involving "domestic abuse, child custody, spousal support, sexual harassment, employment discrimination and other issues of traditional concern to women."

When I left the court in August 1994, the majority went with me, but I must correct Margolick's story in two regards. First, when women justices were in the majority, we did not want to make instant changes in our jurisprudence, only significant changes, and those in a principled way in the proper time and case. Second, as women, we did not dominate the court nor did we want to dominate it. We only wanted our values and the law to relate in a way that would do justice to the law and the people that law serves.

These days the court and the work of the court are behind me. These days I can speak to the St. Croix Valley Branch of the American Association of University Women on "Women and the Power of the Vote" as I did before the 1996 election. The room was full to overflowing, with many high school students present. I felt the old magic of striking a chord that drew us together in common concern. I concluded with Rosabeth Moss Kanter's fifth power of women, the power of persistence. "Hang in," she said. "Instant success takes time. We can't let the heart's energy dissipate."

As I left the building, four girls, tenth graders, stopped me. "You said there were five powers of women. What are the other four?" Now *there* is the future.

BELLA S. ABZUG was born in 1920 and died March 31, 1998. During her lifetime she became one of America's best-known public figures and feminists. A Democrat, she represented a New York district in Congress from 1971 to 1977. She presided over the landmark National Conference on Women in Houston in 1977, and in 1978, President Carter named her as co-chair of the National Advisory Committee for Women. She founded Women USA, a group committed to educating and registering women voters. Over the past twenty years she was actively involved in global women's and environmental issues, and co-founded the Women's Environment and Development Organization (WEDO). She earned a B.A. degree from Hunter College and a J.D. degree from Columbia Law School.

Bella Abzug completed her chapter "Woman Energy" three months before her death.

Woman Energy

BELLA S. ABZUG

I N MY LONG CAREER as a feminist and political activist I have been
called many things, but I do not have an identity problem. I'm also
known as the woman with the hat—and therein lies a story.

When I graduated from Columbia University Law School in the
1940s, only 2 percent of lawyers were women. (My first choice had
been Harvard Law School, but no women were allowed then into
that male legal sanctuary.) My first job was at a New York law firm.
Whenever I was sent to a client's office, I would introduce myself and
give my firm's name. The answer would always be, "Fine, please sit
down." I'd wait and wait, and finally I'd introduce myself all over
again and the answer would always be, "Yes, we know, but we are
waiting." I would ask, "What are we waiting for?" and the answer
would be, "We're waiting for the lawyer."

That's when I had an identity crisis. They assumed I was a clerk or a secretary but certainly not a lawyer. They just weren't used to seeing young women lawyers. I went home and discussed it with my husband, Martin. We figured out that since in those days professional women usually wore hats, I should wear one too. So from then on I wore a hat to work, and my identity problem was solved. After that, when I went to a client's office, they'd know I was there on legal business.

I grew to like wearing hats, and they also became an asset when in 1970, at the age of fifty, I decided to run for the U.S. Congress. As I campaigned in the crowded streets and neighborhoods of Manhattan, my young campaign workers would shout, "Come meet Bella Abzug." People would ask, "Which one is she?" and they'd say, "She's the one with the hat." Then I'd be surrounded and get a chance to make impromptu speeches and answer questions.

My campaign slogan, which has since been used in many election campaigns by women in the United States and around the world, was, "This woman's place is in the House—the House of Representatives." When we celebrated my victory on election night, my older daughter, Eve, said, "Thank God, we got her out of our house and into their House."

When I first entered Congress, my colleagues made a big fuss about my wearing a hat on the House floor. They seemed more interested in what was on my head, rather than what was in it. Finally, I sensed that they wanted me to take my hat off, so I decided to keep it on as my personal declaration of independence. This was an era when cuspidors were on the House floor to accommodate male smokers, the gym was accessible to women members only on a very limited basis, and finding a "ladies room" required a major trek.

Patricia Ireland, president of the National Organization for Women (NOW), recalled in the *Chattanooga Free Press* that a woman's bathroom near the Senate was not installed until 1993. "Now it's within a bladder's distance from the floor. Before that, they had to go to a different floor and use a public bathroom" (December 8, 1996).

The need to get more women into elected and appointive office was a major theme of my campaign. In January 1971, when I came into Congress, there were only ten women out of 435 in the House and one out of a hundred in the U.S. Senate. The numbers have increased significantly since then, but representation of women remains far below the numbers of elected and appointed government posts to which we are entitled as a majority of the population. This gaping hole in our democracy is not because women are not interested.

Foremothers

Women have been organizing politically since the 1830s and the movement to abolish slavery. One hundred and fifty years ago in 1848, the first women's rights meeting was held in Seneca Falls, New York. Elizabeth Cady Stanton, strongly supported by Frederick Douglass, won approval from initially skeptical participants for her proposal that women should demand the right to vote as part of their Declaration of Sentiments.

Looking back in 1926 on their eventually successful suffrage struggle, which culminated with adoption of the Nineteenth Amendment to the Constitution on August 26, 1920, Carrie Chapman Catt wrote in *Woman Suffrage and Politics:* "To get the word 'male' in effect out of the Constitution cost the women of the country 52 years of pauseless campaign. . . . During that time they were forced to conduct 56 campaigns or referenda to male voters; 480 campaigns to get legislatures to submit suffrage amendments to voters; 47 campaigns to get state constitutional conventions to write woman suffrage into state constitutions; 277 campaigns to get state party conventions to include woman suffrage planks; 30 campaigns to get presidential party conventions to adopt woman suffrage planks in party platforms; and 19 campaigns with 19 successive Congresses."

Women who now casually take for granted our right to vote and to run for office should say a silent prayer of thanks to our indefatigable foremothers, and those who don't bother to vote should feel a proper sense of shame.

Even before we won the right to vote, our foremothers were challenging the limitations imposed on women's political aspirations. In 1886, Stanton tested women's constitutional right to run for office by seeking a seat in Congress as an independent candidate, even though there was no women's vote. Of course, she didn't make it.

Under the banner of a party that she created and called the Equal Rights Party, Victoria Claflin Woodhull, a flamboyant feminist of that era, ran for president in 1872, and in 1884, Belva Lockwood, an attorney who had won the right for women to argue cases before the U.S. Supreme Court, ran for president under the banner of the Women's National Equal Rights Party.

It was not until 1917 that Jeannette Rankin, an independent-minded Republican suffragist and pacifist from Montana, became the first woman elected to Congress. She arrived in time to cast the one and only vote against U.S. entry into World War I and lost the next election.

Once suffrage was won in 1920, however, few women sought public office; but male politicians initially were quite responsive to women's demands. The 1920 Democratic platform included twelve of fifteen social policy provisions advocated by the League of Women Voters. Warren Harding, the successful Republican candidate for president, endorsed equal pay for women, an eight-hour day, protective maternity and infant care laws, and creation of a federal department of social welfare. Both parties also named an equal number of men and women to their national committees, a largely ceremonial move that did not admit women to the inner circles of party bosses.

By the mid-1920s, tokenism gave way to the traditional downgrading of women. One explanation was that women were not voting in huge numbers as expected, and those who did appeared to vote like the men in their families. The "gender gap" in electoral voting was still decades away. According to the official report of the 1977 National Conference on Women, former suffragists spent little effort on running for public office, instead devoting their energies to social reform: "The die was cast when the newly organized League of Women Voters decided, after much debate, to concentrate on mobilizing public support behind reform programs and educating women in the tasks of citizenship on a nonpartisan basis. Suffrage leaders went their separate ways, working hard and effectively for a variety of causes."

Power in Public Office

Even with their small numbers, women in Congress made a difference. Jeannette Rankin introduced the first social legislation affecting women and children, which provided funding to reduce the mortality rate among mothers and their newborn infants. Women later played key roles in passing significant laws such as the Fair Labor Standards Act of 1938, the 1963 Equal Pay Act, the 1964 Civil Rights Act, and Title IX of the Education Amendments of 1972.

One of the earliest votes I cast in Congress was to approve the Equal Rights Amendment. I helped write and pass the Freedom of Information and Privacy Acts and the milestone "Government in the Sunshine" law, which for the first time opened up government agencies to public scrutiny.

I also wrote the first law banning discrimination against women in obtaining credit, loans, and mortgages, and introduced precedent-setting bills on comprehensive child care, social security for homemakers, abortion rights, homosexual rights, and rehabilitation and education benefits for Vietnam veterans.

One of my most satisfying memories from my years in Congress, 1971 through 1976, is of the young male veterans injured in Vietnam, a war we should never have entered, who camped out in my office while they lobbied for benefits and reparations. One of my staff members devoted all his time to handling complaints from Vietnam veterans, men as well as women.

Among my final acts in Congress was writing and getting passed a bill authorizing the 1977, first and only, federally funded National Conference on Women. That historic event, which drew an estimated twenty thousand women and men to Houston, was a high point in empowerment for women.

Delegates elected from every state debated, amended, and adopted a National Plan of Action for the Advancement of Women that addressed major needs and concerns of women, including our demand for women's equality in governance. That document serves as a benchmark for the demonstrable gains women have made in our quest for social, political, and economic justice.

But women's entry into elected and appointed government office has been a tortuously slow and at times insulting process. In the early postsuffrage days, about one-third of the women sent to Congress were widows of members. The first woman U.S. senator was Rebecca Felton, an eighty-seven-year-old suffragist from Georgia who was appointed as a token until the regularly elected male senator arrived. She was there for only one day.

Nine years passed before another woman appeared in the Senate, a widow appointee from Arkansas, Hattie Caraway. Until the 1970s, the numbers of women in Congress, the cabinet, other executive posts, and state legislatures remained abysmally small. Some progress has been made, but we're still far from the goal of fifty-fifty, true equality.

Only with formation of the multipartisan National Women's Political Caucus (NWPC) in 1971 did women begin to organize on a nationwide scale to encourage and support women for elective and appointive office and to press for equal representation in the Democratic and Republican parties.

As a co-founder and first co-chair of the NWPC, I was among the handful of women in Congress who focused on our insufficient numbers in policymaking. As a liberal Democrat, I concentrated particularly on getting equal numbers of women into the Democratic National Committee and in state delegations to nominating conventions. Republican women focused similarly on their party.

New women's advocacy groups were formed, among them the Women's Education for Delegate Selection Fund, the Women's Education Fund, the Women's Campaign Fund, and EMILY's List, an acronym for "early money is like yeast"—meaning that funds for women aspirants to elective office have to be raised early and selectively, with the focus on women candidates who have a good chance of winning.

Slowly, with enormous effort, time, and creative strategizing by women's groups, we are getting more women into elective office at every level. Continuing activity by women advocates and the emergence of the powerful gender gap vote signify to me that we can, will, and must have fifty-fifty representation in the beginning years of the twenty-first century.

By 1998, women comprised 21 percent of state legislatures and about 20 percent of municipal offices. Women held fifty-nine seats, or 11.5 percent, in the Congress; 27 percent of them are women of color. Carol Moseley-Braun is the first African American woman senator. Shirley Chisholm (Democrat, New York), who served from 1968 to 1983, was the first African American woman member of the House. We worked together on a number of issues, including child care. The first Asian American woman elected to the House was my dear friend and co-worker, Patsy Mink (Democrat, Hawaii).

Power at the Polls

Emergence of the gender gap in voting was first noted in the 1980 election, when Ronald Reagan won the presidency with 8 percentage points less support from women than from men. In subsequent elections the gap widened. Significant numbers of women were more supportive of Democratic candidates who were considered "good" on women's priority issues, ranging from job and pay equity, health care, child care, family assistance programs, education, and environmental protection to reproductive and sexual rights.

The women's vote was credited with electing President Clinton in 1992 and 1996 and also produced another "first": California's two senators are women, Dianne Feinstein and Barbara Boxer, both Democrats; and Maine's two senators are women, Olympia Snowe and Susan Collins, both Republicans. Feinstein said that issues important to women were more likely to get a careful hearing after the 1996 election. "The big sensitizing factor," she said, "was the gender gap, because it was huge" (*Chattanooga Free Press,* December 8, 1996).

The gender gap is a potent tool for women to use in advancing positive change. One of the most direct ways is for women to come into government in larger numbers than ever before. I am not advocating voting for a woman just because she is a woman. That would be silly, insulting, and unproductive. I like to say, "Vote for a woman who supports . . . ," and then I run down a list of some of the issues that I believe are essential to good government, good public policy, women's rights, and human rights.

I use those criteria not only for the U.S. political scene but also globally. In most countries, women have been largely excluded from political power, whether their countries are considered democracies, plutocracies, or dictatorships.

Global Power

Only a few women head governments at any one time. When last I looked, only seven women headed country delegations to the United Nations. Aside from Eleanor Roosevelt, who, as a U.S. delegation member, led the fight for human rights at the UN, the U.S. has had only two women UN ambassadors: Jeane Kirkpatrick and, most recently, Madeleine K. Albright, who became the first woman Secretary of State. This happened only after women's rights activists transformed the rumor that Albright was just a "second-tier" possibility for the post into the reality of her highly popular appointment.

Worldwide, women have only a toehold on decision-making positions. According to the UN, as of January 1996 the number of female cabinet ministers had doubled in the last decade to almost 7 percent, but forty-eight countries had no women cabinet members. What some consider a "critical mass"—30 percent women at the ministerial level—was achieved in only five small countries: Barbados, Finland, Liechtenstein, Seychelles, and Sweden.

Ten nations, including Austria, Denmark, Ireland, Netherlands, Norway, and three Caribbean islands, reported 20 to 29 percent women as ministers. In Asia, the Pacific region, and Eastern Europe, the proportion of women in cabinet positions was less than 5 percent. In all the parliaments of the world, women comprise less than 10 percent of the members.

At the UN itself, equality for women in employment has not been achieved. Words are easier to get from the UN than deeds, but under continuing pressure from women within the UN secretariat and the increasingly effective women's groups from civil society, the General Assembly has reaffirmed its goal of 50 percent women overall in jobs by the year 2000, subject to geographical distribution. It has also recommitted itself to appointing more women to senior decision-making positions.

Within the global UN system, more women are being appointed or elected to high-ranking posts. In 1997, Mary Robinson, former president of the Irish republic, was elected to head the UN Commission on Human Rights. Although the Irish presidency is largely ceremonial, Robinson describes her election in 1991 as "the psychic equivalent of the collapse of the Berlin wall," and attributes it to the power of women. She has said that when women lead, they change institutions; in working toward their goals, women tend to operate with a sense of community and a leadership style that is open, flexible, and compassionate.

As more women come into political leadership, from local communities to the topmost positions, we are seeing the products of a virtual explosion of activity by women around the world. That forward motion began with the first UN-sponsored global women's conference in Mexico City in 1975 and flowered at the huge 1995 Fourth World Conference on Women in Beijing.

Woman Energy

I attended all the UN conferences on women, including Copenhagen in 1980 and Nairobi in 1985. Since 1991, I have been at almost every major UN conference, including those on the environment, population, and social and economic concerns.

But I became most deeply involved when, in November 1991, a group that I co-founded with Mim Kelber—the Women's Environment and Development Organization (WEDO)—convened the First World Women's Congress for a Healthy Planet, in preparation for the 1992 UN Earth Summit in Rio. A rousing success, the congress was attended by fifteen hundred women from eighty-four countries, including many who had never been out of their countries before or been involved in UN matters.

After hearing testimony presented to a tribunal of five women judges, all of us together created our own Women's Action Agenda 21. That report became our guide to amending Agenda 21, the document that was to emerge from the Earth Summit. We defined a healthy and sustainable environment as dependent on the empowerment of women and "contingent on world peace, human rights, participatory democracy, the self-determination of peoples, respect for indigenous people and their lands, cultures, and traditions, and the protection of all species."

We demanded our right "as half the world's population, to bring our perspectives, values, skills, and experiences into policymaking, on an equal basis with men, not only at the UN Conference on Environment and Development in June 1992 but on into the twenty-first century."

The collaborative process we used was very similar to the way women members of Congress had acted when I was there, and the way they still do. We picked our issues, we caucused, we researched and wrote amendments to bills, we lobbied our colleagues for support, and sometimes we succeeded.

Leading up to Rio, we introduced the methodology of the women's caucus to the UN conference process. Women NGOs (nongovernmental organizations) from every region and from a broad range of "issues groups" worked on proposed language changes in the official UN documents, set priorities, and met with official delegates to seek support for our proposed amendments. We succeeded in transforming the document from one that barely mentioned women into a model gender-sensitive and gender-friendly document that was approved by the heads of state gathered at the Rio conference.

This participatory approach was so effective that the women's caucus has become an institution at every major UN conference since Rio—the human rights conference in Vienna, the population conference in Cairo, the social summit in Copenhagen, and the 1995 women's conference in Beijing.

A majority of the official delegates at the Beijing conference were women; even more impressive were the twenty thousand women who traveled by planes, ships, trains, and buses to attend the parallel NGO forum. Among them were seven thousand American women of every age, class, color, and interest group.

When I looked at a list of the U.S. women, I was delighted to find out how many were names unfamiliar to me—and I thought I knew most of our feminist activists! Beijing was an "it changed my life" experience for many of the women who came, and has become an inspiring guide to the kind of world we seek for all people in the twenty-first century.

The spontaneous combustion of woman energy at the largest gathering in UN history is building a movement to propel political, economic, social, cultural, and spiritual transformation. The new century must be the first to declare the end of global gender apartheid and all forms of oppression. It is the time for recognizing that all issues are "women's issues."

Around the world and here in the United States, women are organizing and speaking out on all the urgent issues of our time. We see them on television, in our communities and countries. We know that even the United States, as powerful as it is, increasingly reflects the disparities of a world in moral, economic, and political conflict.

The Platform for Action adopted by consensus of 185 governments at Beijing is not perfect, but if its visionary recommendations were transformed from paper to reality, we could welcome the new century with hope, joy, and certainty of a better future for our families, our loved ones, and our world.

We have the vision, and women in large numbers around the world are working to make it a reality. Women in the United States have developed their own National Action Agenda, based on the Beijing mandate and women's conferences held in almost every state in 1996. The President's Inter-Agency Council, consisting of representatives from every federal department and agency, is working on implementing a range of commitments made by President Clinton. They fall short of the Beijing Platform for Action and the U.S. Women's National Action Agenda but, limited as they are, most of them represent progress for women.

Having worked in the women's movement, the peace movement, the legal system, the Congress, and the UN community for most of my life, I have faith in women's transformational politics.

We don't simply want to join the establishment. We want to change it. We are not interested in just joining a "polluted stream." We want to change the stagnant waters into a fresh-flowing stream, making it safe and green and life-enhancing for everyone. We want to make it flow in new directions, and that is why we struggle for an equal place at the table, in city hall, in Congress, in international institutions, in the back rooms, and in front rooms wherever decisions are made about how we live and how we die.

Our movement has arms that reach out to women everywhere. We have legs that take us to the places where policies are decided, and, most of all, we have brains to figure out how to use our collective strength to make the Earth a safe, friendly, nurturing place for all living things.

One final question: If you agree with the above, when did you last let your elected representatives know your views, and have you ever considered running for office yourself?

OLYMPIA J. SNOWE (Republican, Maine) was elected to the U.S. Senate in 1994. She served in the House of Representatives for eight terms. When she was first elected to Congress in 1978 at the age of thirty-one, she was the youngest Republican woman and first Greek American woman elected to Congress. Snowe has won more federal elections in Maine than any other candidate since World War II. She was first elected to the Maine House of Representatives in 1973 to the seat vacated by the death of her husband, and in 1976 she was elected to the state senate. She is a member of the Senate Committee on Commerce, Science and Transportation, where she chairs the Subcommittee on Oceans and Fisheries. Snowe also serves on the Senate Committees on the Armed Services, the Budget, and Small Business. She is a graduate of the University of Maine at Orono.

Up from Silence

OLYMPIA J. SNOWE

I GREW UP IN A TOWN where politics was passion—Maine's state capital of Augusta. Throughout that central Maine community, the happenings at Maine's statehouse were a focus of the day, and each of my parents—my mother a daughter of immigrants, my father an immigrant himself—worked in a job that had close and easy access to the politicians of the day. Others remember me accompanying my mother as she visited the statehouse, or my father to his job as a cook at his State Street Diner, where I would playfully spy on the Maine politicos. I spent my earliest years in this exciting setting.

When I was eight, my mother died at the age of thirty-nine of breast cancer. I remember watching my father struggle with a tremendous burden as a single parent. He sent me to St. Basil's Academy, a Greek Orthodox school in Garrison, New York, and I remember writing to him every day because I knew how difficult life had become for him. When my father died of heart disease just one year later, I went to live with my aunt and uncle and their five children. My aunt worked in a factory and my uncle was a barber. After my uncle died shortly thereafter, my aunt had to support us.

I learned from the tragedies that shaped my life. My mother, in a letter to a friend, described the ravages of breast cancer, confronted the ultimate prospect of her death, and wondered what would become of her husband and children. Years later, I can look back and understand the extent to which my mother's death from breast cancer—and the indelible mark that this dreaded disease left on my life—would shape the nature of the work I would eventually pursue in the United States Congress to improve women's health.

When I first came to Washington in January 1979 as the U.S. representative from Maine's Second Congressional District, it became clear to me rather quickly that Congress was practically oblivious to a critical set of issues: those of particular importance to women.

That first year I came to Congress, the youngest Republican woman ever elected, I was one of only seventeen women in the U.S. House and Senate. That was less than 3 percent of the entire Congress—in a nation in which women made up 54 percent of the electorate.

Women across the nation had for years asked their members of Congress, most of them men, to act on issues of importance to women and their families. For too long, women in America were the great "silent majority": we were the majority of voters, yet our calls for action on the women's health agenda were too often met with silence.

It was only when women ascended to take their place in the halls of Congress that these issues finally found their voice—issues like women's health care, child care, child support, sexual harassment, and domestic violence. Early on in my tenure in Congress I recognized, as one of the few women representatives, that I had a major obligation—in fact, a responsibility—to raise these issues to the top of our national legislative agenda.

The Congressional Caucus for Women's Issues

I found reassurance in the Congressional Caucus for Women's Issues, founded just two years before by Republican Representative Margaret Heckler of Massachusetts and Democratic Representative Elizabeth Holtzman of New York, to advance legislation of importance to the women in the House of Representatives. Their mission was to work on a bipartisan basis on issues that united them, rather than divided them, issues that required altering laws to reflect women's changing role in society and their dual responsibilities of work and family. I joined the caucus when I entered Congress in 1979, and became co-chair in 1983, where I served until my election to the U.S. Senate in 1994.

Perhaps it was due to my mother's untimely death from breast cancer or my experience watching other women grapple with their health care needs, but the inequities facing women in health care shaped my time as caucus co-chair. For too many years, women's health care needs were ignored or poorly understood, and women were systematically excluded from important health research.

As the daughter of a woman who lost her battle with breast cancer, I was outraged by the approach that the government and the medical establishment took toward breast cancer and other illnesses that affect women. One famous medical study on breast cancer examined hundreds of men. Another federally funded study examined the ability of aspirin to prevent heart attacks in twenty thousand medical doctors, all of whom were men, despite the fact that heart disease is the leading cause of death among women. Knowledge about appropriate courses of treatment for women lagged far behind that for men for many diseases. Research into diseases that predominately affected women, such as breast cancer, went grossly underfunded.

But that was before women members brought the vital issue of women's health to the fore. As co-chairs of the caucus in 1989, Representative Pat Schroeder and I, along with Representative Henry Waxman, called for a General Accounting Office investigation into the inclusion of women and minorities in medical research at the National Institutes of Health. This study documented the widespread exclusion of women from medical research and spurred the caucus in 1990 to introduce the first Women's Health Equity Act (WHEA)—landmark legislation on women's health. This comprehensive legislation provided Congress with its first broad, forward-looking health agenda designed to redress the historical inequities that women face in medical research, prevention, and treatment services.

Since the initial introduction of WHEA, we have made important strides on behalf of women's health. Legislation from that first package became law in June 1993, mandating the inclusion of women and minorities in clinical trials at the National Institutes of Health (NIH). We secured dramatic funding increases for research into breast cancer, osteoporosis, and cervical cancer, and my legislation established the Office of Research on Women's Health at NIH. In 1996, Congress enacted the Mothers and Newborns Health Protection Act, which will end the practice of "drive-through deliveries," whereby hospitals discharge mothers within hours of delivery.

Equality in Women's Health

Despite these achievements, women remain at a stark and singular disadvantage in the health care system and in health research. Equality in women's health remains a goal, not a completed task, and we still have a long way to go. For example, physicians are more than twice as likely to perceive that the same disease affects men more seriously than women. A recent study by the Commonwealth Fund found that more women than men failed to receive the care they needed and that about one-third of the women surveyed did not have any basic preventive services: a pap smear, a clinical breast exam, a pelvic exam, or a complete physical exam. Women also reported greater communication problems with their physicians.

Doctors are less likely to diagnose heart disease in women than in men with the same symptoms. Moreover, women receive less aggressive treatment than men for heart disease, thus accounting for why the disease remains the number-one killer of women. Not surprisingly, women have been greatly underrepresented in studies of the risk factors, patterns, and treatment options for heart disease.

This story is repeated again and again for other illnesses that predominantly affect women. There is no known cure for breast cancer, little is known about prevention, and treatment options are few in number. Cervical and ovarian cancer present a major threat to American women. And osteoporosis, a debilitating bone disease, strikes twenty-eight million Americans, 80 percent of whom are women. Although this disease causes tremendous suffering and often results in a loss of independence for elderly women, many women remain unaware that osteoporosis can often be prevented and treated.

As more and more women play a role in our legislative system (in the 105th Congress we numbered fifty-two in the House and nine in the Senate), legislators have an opportunity to work together on a bipartisan basis to take the next crucial steps toward achieving equity. Improving the health of American women requires a far greater understanding of women's health needs and conditions, and ongoing evaluation in the areas of research, education, prevention, treatment, and the delivery of services. In recent years, I have focused my work on women's health in several key areas—most notably, breast cancer. I am working to ensure that one day, no young girl or boy will ever have to lose a mother to this dreaded disease.

There is no question that breast cancer is one of the major public health crises facing this nation. In 1997 alone, physicians diagnosed 180,000 new cases of breast cancer in this country, and more than forty-four thousand women died from the disease. Breast cancer is the most common form of cancer and the second leading cause of cancer deaths among American women. As we continue to wage war against this deadly disease, we have our work cut out for us. In 1955, when I lost my mother, about one in fourteen women developed breast cancer in their lifetime. After years of research and increased knowledge, the number today is more than one in eight.

Research Breakthroughs

Despite these daunting statistics, there is now cause for hope. Scientists have made encouraging progress in recent years in the fight to conquer breast cancer. Researchers have isolated the genes responsible for some forms of inherited breast cancer, and are beginning to understand the mechanism of the cancer cell itself. To capitalize upon these advances and to support scientists investigating this disease, we must enhance federal funding for research. Already, we have boosted such funding from $100 million in 1991 to more than $500 million in 1996.

In 1997, I introduced a bill to increase the funding authorization level for breast cancer research to an unprecedented $590 million. This funding level, which scientists believe is necessary for progress in fighting this disease, will contribute substantially toward solving the mysteries surrounding breast cancer.

In addition to increasing funding for breast cancer research, improving access to mammograms and other early detection methods is one of my top legislative priorities. That is why I took swift action early in 1997 when an advisory panel to the National Cancer Institute (NCI) decided against recommending that women in their forties seek routine mammograms, despite compelling new scientific evidence that routine screening for women in this age group could reduce death rates. After the Senate unanimously approved my resolution urging NCI to revisit this issue, it changed its position and endorsed routine mammograms.

Breakthroughs in genetic research promise to further revolutionize treatment of breast cancer and other aspects of women's health. Progress in the field of genetics is accelerating at a breathtaking rate. As a result, researchers are increasingly able to identify predispositions to certain diseases (based on genetic testing), and to treat and manage such diseases successfully. This holds tremendous promise for the approximately fifteen million people affected by over four thousand currently known genetic disorders, and the millions more who are carriers of genetic diseases and who may pass them on to their children.

As a woman with a history of breast cancer in her family, I am delighted with the possibilities for further treatment advances based on the recent discovery of two genes related to breast cancer—BRCA1 and BRCA2. Women who inherit the mutated forms of either gene have an 85 percent risk of developing breast cancer in their lifetimes and a 50 percent risk of developing ovarian cancer.

Although there are no known preventive measures to offer women with the mutated breast cancer gene to ensure that they do not develop the disease, genetic testing makes it possible for carriers of these mutated genes to take extra precautions—such as mammograms and self-examinations—in order to detect cancer at its earliest stage.

Genetic Discrimination

The tremendous promise of genetic testing, however, is being significantly threatened by insurers that use the results of genetic testing to deny or limit coverage to consumers. In fact, a recent survey of individuals with a known genetic condition in the family revealed that 22 percent had been denied health insurance coverage because of genetic information.

In addition to the potentially devastating consequences of insurers using genetic information to deny health insurance, the *fear* of discrimination has equally harmful consequences for consumers and for scientific research. For example, many women, who would probably take extra precautions if they knew they had the mutant breast cancer gene, might not seek testing for fear of losing their health insurance.

Patients may be afraid to disclose information about their genetic status to their physicians, thus hindering treatment or preventive efforts. People may be unwilling to participate in potentially ground-breaking research because they fear revealing information about their genetic status. In recent studies at the National Institutes of Health, 32 percent of the women offered genetic testing for breast cancer declined to take it. The overwhelming majority of those who refused to take the test cited concerns about health insurance discrimination and loss of privacy as the reason.

The Kassebaum-Kennedy Health Insurance Reform Act of 1996 took the critical first step in protecting Americans against genetic discrimination by ensuring that people who change jobs cannot lose their health insurance based on genetic information. In order to provide more comprehensive protections against genetic discrimination, New York Representative Louise Slaughter and I introduced broader legislation in the 105th Congress that prevents insurers from charging higher premiums based on genetic information, prohibits insurers from disclosing genetic information without a person's written consent, and also applies protections against genetic discrimination to Medigap coverage.

Prevention

To succeed in broadening our approach to women's health, we must focus not only on diagnosing and treating illnesses that affect women but also on providing care to prevent health problems before they occur. To do that, we must improve health insurance coverage for women and reduce out-of-pocket health costs. That is why I introduced the Equity in Prescription Insurance and Contraceptive Coverage Act (EPICC) in 1997 to improve access to prescription contraceptives—a basic part of women's health care. Although almost all health care plans cover prescription drugs and devices, most of these plans treat prescription contraceptives very differently. According to a 1994 study by the Alan Guttmacher Institute, only half of large group insurance plans cover prescription contraceptives, and only one-third cover oral contraceptives, the most popular form of birth control.

The lack of contraceptive coverage in health insurance has important public health and economic consequences for women in this country. By helping families to space their pregnancies adequately, contraceptives contribute to healthy pregnancies and healthy births and reduce rates of maternal complications and low birth-weight.

Unfortunately, the lack of contraceptive coverage means that economic constraints may force women to use less expensive and less effective contraceptives, thus leading to unintended pregnancies and abortions. Lack of coverage also helps account for why women pay 68 percent more than men in out-of-pocket health care costs. It does not make sense that so many otherwise insured women cannot afford access to the most effective contraceptives because of this disparity in coverage, nor does it make sense that under many of today's health insurance plans, a woman can afford a prescription to alleviate an allergy symptom but not a prescription to prevent an unintended, life-altering pregnancy.

The approach of my bill is simple. It says that health plans that provide coverage of prescription drugs cannot carve out prescription contraceptives for less extensive coverage. Similarly, plans that cover outpatient medical services cannot limit or exclude the counseling or medical services necessary for effective contraceptive use. The bill does not require special treatment of contraceptives, just that they be treated on a par with other prescription drugs.

The need for this legislation is clear. Every year there are 3.6 million unintended pregnancies in this country—over 56 percent of all pregnancies—and half will end in abortion. These are staggering statistics. But what is even more staggering is that it does not have to be this way. If prescription contraceptives were covered like other prescription drugs, many more Americans could afford to use safe, effective means to prevent unintended pregnancies.

As I think back to my mother's experience and review the recent gains we have made in women's health, I am excited about what the future holds for women across this nation. I look forward to a future where the health care community will *accommodate* women's biological differences, not ignore them; where we will be treated as equals in medical research, not as an afterthought; and where our daughters and granddaughters will be able to expect the very best in health care research, funding, and treatment and not have to settle for second best. But one vision is certain: never again will women be a missing page from America's medical textbook.

CARMEN DELGADO VOTAW is the director of public policy
for United Way of America, and from 1991 to 1997 was director of government relations for the Girl Scouts of the U.S.A.
She was chief of staff from 1985 to 1991 to Representative
Jaime B. Fuster (Democrat, Puerto Rico) and was vice president of Information and Services for Latin America (ISLA)
from 1981 to 1984. Formerly she was president of the Inter
American Commission of Women in the Organization of
American States. Votaw is the past president of the National
Conference of Puerto Rican Women, former vice president of
the Overseas Education Fund of the League of Women Voters,
and was co-chair of the presidential National Advisory Committee for Women. She is author of the bilingual *Puerto Rican
Women* (1995). She holds a B.A. degree from American University and an honorary doctorate from Hood College.

Face to Face with Power

CARMEN DELGADO VOTAW

G LORIA STEINEM CALLED IT the "Tuesday Massacre." It came in the aftermath of a tense hour-and-a-half meeting of the National Advisory Committee for Women with President Jimmy Carter on January 12, 1979.

Late that afternoon, members of the committee—appointed on June 20, 1978, by the president of the United States through executive order #12050—walked out of the White House onto the driveway for a scheduled press conference. A snow-covered lawn presaged the two feet of snow that would make the nation's capital look like a fairyland by the next morning.

As our boots sank into the inhospitable landscape, a sense of foreboding hung in the air as though the tenseness of the meeting inside was slowly drifting outside to envelop us like the snow.

A carefully crafted half-hour meeting with President Carter had rambled on in spite of the iron-grip approach I had planned, as co-chair of the committee, to ensure we would cover all the points we needed to convey. This was our moment to present the president of the United States with an assessment of progress made on implementing the National Plan of Action for the Advancement of Women. The plan had been adopted at the historic National Conference on Women held in Houston the previous year.

The committee dared to have opinions on the financial picture of the nation and its effects on women, including military expenditures, which we believed sapped the country's commitment to the poor and to women's advancement. We were venturing into issue areas that women were not expected to discuss; economic policy, jobs, and poverty were not supposed to be "women's issues."

Although well intended, the president's proposed anti-inflation programs would impose disproportionate burdens on women, the committee argued. Such policies might cause unemployment to rise, slash social and human needs programs, postpone comprehensive national health insurance, and leave poverty and the financial plight of the cities unaddressed.

The committee echoed the dictum of the president's assistant, Stuart Eizenstat, that the increasing participation of women in the labor force would have profound implications on the nation's public policy. We added that the administration had not "sensitized itself" to the issue and was "negligent" in failing to develop an enlightened approach that fully appreciated women's changing role in the economy.

At that point in our history, 49 percent of women were in the labor force, 50 percent were not employed, but 90 percent had worked outside the home for some periods of their lives. Women were 63 percent of the sixteen million Americans living below the poverty level; black and other ethnic origin women were 20 percent of the poor.

The national unemployment rate stood at 7 percent for women, as compared to 5 percent for men; unemployment for minority women was twice as high as for white women. Among minority teenage women, it was a disturbing 36.8 percent.

Women were segregated into low-paying occupations, with 80 percent clustered at the bottom of the pay scale. For the prior twenty years, the wage gap between women and men had remained unchanged, with women averaging sixty cents an hour for every dollar earned by men. There were not enough job training programs for working or unemployed women, displaced homemakers, minority women, disabled women, and women on welfare.

Antidiscriminatory laws and executive orders designed to help women break out of their occupational ghettos were inadequately enforced. Aggressive enforcement was particularly needed to overcome the chilling effects of the 1978 U.S. Supreme Court decision in *Regents of the University of California* v. *Bakke,* a landmark affirmative action case.

Day-care centers were available for only 2 percent of the six million preschool-age children of working mothers. Millions of minority women, in addition to bearing the burden of discrimination, suffered disproportionately from poverty, unemployment, low-paying jobs, inadequate health and maternity services, and poor education and housing.

Older women, a majority of our senior citizens, had a median income of $2,800 a year, half the income of men in their age group. Five million disabled women suffered special discrimination in their search for education, job training, employment, and independence. Poverty afflicted higher than average numbers of the thirty-four million women then living on farms, in migrant camps and rural areas, or on Indian reservations.

The committee pleaded for the unmet needs and aspirations of women. We stressed that "what happens to us affects the whole nation" and called for the "national agenda to achieve women's full rights and equality."

We wanted recognition as "full participants with the administration in setting national priorities, developing public policy, and determining budget allocations and expenditures." That was a tall order for any president to bear, but in reality it was what the energized women's movement was indeed demanding. Benign neglect was not in the committee's lexicon.

A bone of contention was the proposal by the administration for voluntary wage guidelines that limited wage gains to 7 percent. We opposed cuts in jobs programs including those in public service. Reductions in funds for displaced homemakers, vocational education, job research and evaluation, welfare demonstration projects, and the enforcement of antidiscrimination statutes were all part and parcel of the "insensitivity" toward women noted by the committee.

The committee capped its litany about federal budget cuts with two issues that would not cost taxpayers a cent: the ratification of the Equal Rights Amendment and the appointment of more women as federal judges. At the time, few women served on the federal bench and President Carter had made a commitment to appoint more women. The president had also been supportive of the Equal Rights Amendment; the question was how much of a priority and muscle could be brought to bear to secure the final three states needed to clinch final ratification.

The Houston Mandate

Raising consciousness was the committee's sacred commitment; echoing the entreaty of Abigail Adams to her husband, John, to "remember the ladies." Magnified by the press and publicity that always followed Bella Abzug, our call became "remember the women because we are not an appendage to this nation. We are part of its heart and soul. We are, with men, its central characters. Women's place indeed is every place."

Fueled by our charge to "advise the president on the implementation of the Plan of Action" and armed with data on how poorly women were doing in key planks of the plan approved in Houston, I primed the committee on how to make the best use of our meeting.

We had been allotted thirty minutes by Hamilton Jordan, the president's principal assistant. Weeks earlier the committee had rejected an offer of a fifteen-minute meeting. After trying for months to meet with the president, the committee believed a fifteen-minute meeting would be just a photo opportunity without substance for the forty people, including three men, who represented a cross section of women's interests.

We believed our committee spoke with the force of not only a presidential mandate but also the legitimacy of thousands of women who had entrusted to us the sacred mission of ensuring that the Plan of Action to achieve women's equality was implemented. The most diverse group of women ever assembled came together in Houston. They had been elected as representatives from their home states under a law passed by Congress at the behest of former Representative Abzug. Our mandate was a direct mandate from the people.

When the committee declined unanimously to meet with the president for a mere fifteen minutes after so many cajoling calls to the White House, most of us, including me, did not realize how impertinent or unusual it was to say no. In fact, we found out it had never happened before.

Babes in arms we were not, but naivete lurked in our veins. A second offer for a half-hour meeting came after a phone call Bella and I had with the president. We explained that we had simply requested more time and meant no disrespect for the presidency. We were swimming in uncharted waters.

What were the issues we had so painstakingly staked out and lovingly crafted to make a concise, yet eloquent, presentation that would get us favorable presidential intervention and understanding? The salient issues were, of course, the ERA, federal judgeships, and the economy in all its manifestations.

At a pre–White House meeting, from which Bella, detained temporarily in New York, was absent, I reviewed the committee members' presentations with them, including length (no longer than three minutes), points to cover, and the action we desired of the president.

My pen would go up or down as a signal when their time was up so that we could cover all our pending issues. I explained the process to Bella during a hurried taxi ride to the White House from the Department of Labor, where our offices were housed.

The debacle commenced when we saw the top leadership of the labor movement march in ahead of us for a meeting with the president. Labor was quite unhappy with the president because of his stance on wage guidelines. They were somber when they came out of their meeting.

A Fateful Meeting

Finally, our long anticipated opportunity began to unfold as we were ushered into the room, with its long table and austere decor, where the cabinet meets. Sitting to the president's left, I had a commanding view of the distinguished, intelligent, dedicated individuals who made up the committee: Lane Kirkland, president of the AFL/CIO; Ellie Smeal, president of the National Organization for Women (NOW); Nancy Neuman, vice president of the League of Women Voters; Erma Bombeck, the writer; Mary Crisp, co-chair of the Republican National Committee; and so many other outstanding women.

What a triumph it seemed. We had been empowered by our sisters across the United States to be their advocates speaking with one voice for the claims we had on our society's resources. A sense of pride and awe was evident as our eyes contemplated the scene. We were well prepared to make our case for more presidential support for our cause. We knew our president to be a firm believer in equality for women. We were poised for a leap into another decade that would become known as the "Decade for Women."

Someone suggested we each introduce ourselves to the president, who had not met with our committee before. There went nearly twelve minutes of our precious time, so the litany of our issues had to be compressed and came up short, with two or three topics waiting to be introduced when a presidential assistant came to advise the president he had to move on.

Until that point he had listened politely, almost mutely, to our monologues. He asked whether we wanted him to respond to the issues presented or continue listening to the scheduled speakers. Of course, we chose the former option and he enumerated the administration's good intentions and record of accomplishments such as the appointment of women to judgeships, which was indeed one of the most notable legacies of the Carter presidency.

However, he said, as the veins of his neck visibly inflated with tension, our committee was confrontational, and we went to the press to air issues without giving him an opportunity to study and respond. He would like to have a more collaborative relationship with us. The time was up; it was time for us to move on and regroup.

Bella seized the opportunity to say how unfair it was to say we were not collaborative; we had not had any access to the president. The committee had been licensed by his executive order, but we had to hunt for resources even to exist. She related that she and I had had to beg and scrounge for staff to help us and for the Department of Labor to house us and do the printing of our newsletter. (Alexis Herman, then director of the Women's Bureau, now President Clinton's secretary of labor, was instrumental in helping us negotiate the labyrinth of the federal bureaucracy so our committee could fulfill its mandate. While Bella lived in New York, I, a resident of Bethesda, Maryland, was the daily general factotum, an unpaid, full-time volunteer doing the work of the committee and of the women of the United States with a small but very capable staff.)

My pen could not contain Bella during the meeting with the president. Unknown hands slipped a note to me: "See Hamilton Jordan before you go." Unbeknownst to me, a similar note was also given to Bella, scheduled for a different time. When she learned about my meeting, she demanded from a startled assistant to Jordan that we be allowed to go together. No, was the terse answer. Something was in the offing; we could tell.

Meanwhile, members of the news media waited in the driveway for our press conference.

The Firing of Bella Abzug

I was told that Bella was going to be asked to resign by Jordan and Eizenstat. I inquired why, told Jordan that the refused fifteen-minute meeting had been a unanimous decision by the committee members and not a capricious ploy by Bella and that she had not even participated in the preparatory meeting to the visit with the president. But my arguments were to no avail.

I was asked to stay on the committee and was given until the following day to make my decision before Bella's firing was announced. This decision was crucial to me, to many others, and to the women's movement.

The Tuesday Massacre was a turning point for me, a Puerto Rican woman of humble origin, born on the southeastern side of a small island with 3.5 million citizens in the Caribbean, raised in the community-spirited town of Yabucoa, Puerto Rico, among the cane fields near the ocean. It was a turning point because it afforded me the opportunity to test my mettle.

How heavy the power of the presidency weighs when the eyes of the nation are focused on actions that have a clear import—on your values, your identity, and your capacity to advocate for the causes dear to your heart. How important it was for me then to recall that the security of my identity came from a long line of proud people descended from the Spaniards, the Taino Indians, and the Africans who came to till the soil that produced sugar cane, which was the mainstay of the Puerto Rican economy at the turn of the last century.

My identity had been nurtured by teachers, whom we held in high esteem when I was growing up. Both my father, Luis Oscar Delgado, and my mother, Candida Paz, were teachers, my own as well as other students' in the third and fifth grades. I could roam my hilly, picturesque town and everybody knew me: "There goes Carmencita," who always got a report card adorned by A's.

I look back on that long night of uncertainty when Bella and I, along with loyal members of our staff, made telephone calls to our supporters across the nation to consult and share what had transpired. Many committee members had left to catch planes and trains, fearing that the steadily increasing accumulation of snow might strand them in Washington. They did not know of the ultimatum handed down to Bella by Jordan and presidential counsel Robert Lipshutz, who reportedly had cautioned Bella not to accuse the administration of discrimination against her because she is Jewish.

Most committee members were supportive: most resigned in solidarity. My choice was clear: resign from the committee with dignity or be forever ostracized by the women's movement.

Standing on Principle

So the die was cast: principle over expediency, commitment to women's causes over entree into the halls of "real" power, being true to myself over courting a possible future of acclaim and recognition.

Making the decision was not as hard as composing a letter of resignation on my typewriter at home in the early hours of the next day, tears streaming down my face, after driving three staff members to their homes late at night in the cottony snow following our frantic evening of telephoning at the office.

I wanted to deliver the letter to the White House before I appeared at a hastily called press conference later that morning at the Mayflower Hotel on Connecticut Avenue, blocks from the White House. The distance I had traveled from the comforting greenery of my native island to the inhospitable cold of Washington, D.C., seemed very far indeed.

The committee disbanded with sore hearts and renewed commitment that we would continue to wage the never-ending battle for the advancement of women in the United States. Sarah Weddington, the president's assistant from Texas who had argued in favor of legalizing abortion before the U.S. Supreme Court in *Roe* v. *Wade,* was charged with assembling another committee. This time the committee would be advisory to the president, but have no newsletter, no mandate for implementation, and no independent voice. Sarah later told me that sacks and sacks of letters predominantly in support of the renegade committee's actions had been received at the White House.

The press—kind and unkind—embellished their reports about the debacle. I, always in the shadow of Bella's big brimmed hats, shared the limelight a bit. The astonished Hispanic press portrayed me as a "profile in courage," the little David aiming a sling with a minute pebble at the presidency. *Nuestro* magazine's headline portrayed me shouting, "I shall not be silenced." The *Miami Herald* proclaimed, "Jolt to Women: Episode Must Not Hamper the Cause of Women." The *New York Times* described the incident in detail with a front-page story on Sunday, January 14, 1979.

The penalty for such brazen behavior was not too heavy to bear. After all, I was not paid—the glory and recognition of the job I held were scant, and the rewards for fulfilling my commitment to women were more psychological than actual. So why did I feel this was a Pyrrhic victory for principle and for my own value system? Why is this a cautionary tale?

Strategically speaking, the grandstanding did not gain us anything in terms of women's advancement, except the sense that principle can be the guiding force for women's behavior no matter what is at stake. It did not position us to influence the implementation of the plan of action, and it did weaken the government machinery created to foster women's advancement.

To date, no committee has had the possibilities we had. There is now no national committee for women, only an intragovernment task force on women, which is entirely constituted of government employees. Nongovernment representatives cannot attend its meetings even as auditors. All meetings of our committee were open to the public, and we engaged in a great deal of consultation and collaboration with all sectors of the women's movement.

Strategic planning for one's career, for accomplishing public policy goals, for implementing a well thought out course of action, as our National Plan of Action for the Advancement of Women was, depends on integrity and commitment to principle. The women's movement has not taken the road well traveled in its quest for equality; instead, it has mapped out other ways to achieve the prized goals of equity and full participation in decision making at all levels.

My turn on the road came up suddenly and opened up new vistas that helped me decide what roles I wanted to play, what commitments I wanted to keep, and where I wanted to diverge from some of the patterns of sisterhood I had experienced.

I also took the road less traveled to find a sense of inner power, not in order to contravene authority but to deeply scan what my values are and where they come from. What price was I willing to pay for short-term gains? Was I willing to compromise a lifelong promise to do everything to ensure that women's voices rise loudly and sonorously on behalf of those elusive goals we continue to pursue into the next century? Caution must not be forgotten; it must be treasured as an opportunity to know ourselves and to ourselves be true.

EVA M. CLAYTON is the First Congressional District Representative for North Carolina. A Democrat, she made history in November 1992 when she became the first African American woman elected to Congress from North Carolina. Her peers elected her as chair of the Democratic freshman class in the 103rd Congress, the first woman ever to hold that post. She is a former member of the Warren County (North Carolina) Board of Commissioners, where she served as chair from 1982 to 1990. She is a former president and board member of the Housing Assistance Council, an elder in her local church, and a member of the Alpha Kappa Alpha sorority. She holds a B.A. degree from Johnson C. Smith University and an M.S. degree from North Carolina Central University.

Expanding Our Horizons

EVA M. CLAYTON

WHEN I WAS A CHILD I dreamed of becoming a medical missionary like Albert Schweitzer. Reading about his work inspired me to want to work in Africa and heal people, as Schweitzer had done. As a medical missionary, I thought, I could combine my religious convictions with a career as a doctor.

My interest in medicine was sparked initially by the difficulties of my friend and neighbor who was crippled by polio. I wanted to help her and others like her. Although I have strayed from my desire to become a medical missionary, as a member of Congress I believe I am doing as much good for other people as I wanted to when I was young.

Both my parents encouraged me to fulfill my aspirations. My mother was the director of an orphanage, a seamstress, and a teacher. Her jobs exposed me to children who were not as fortunate as I was.

I met children who had no parents or material possessions. Even though they didn't have parents, I thought they were blessed to have my mother as their advocate. My mother was a very strong woman, a woman of substance and integrity. She believed in herself and what she was doing, and she believed in me. I am in no small part what I am today because of my parents' strength.

I also loved and admired my father. He was a regional insurance salesman, which was a very important job. He did not have a great formal education, but he was smart, hardworking, and intuitive, and he always made the best of what he had.

I was born in Savannah and grew up in Augusta, Georgia. When I reached college age, I wanted to see parts of the country other than the segregated South I was used to. My parents allowed me to leave home for an American Friends Service Committee (AFSC) summer program that took me to the North. Because it was sponsored by Quakers, a very reputable group of people, my very religious parents thought it would be safe for me to go.

I spent three summers with the AFSC program; those summers changed my life. They enlarged my sense of the world by giving me a global perspective and expanded my intellectual development. I discovered pluralism by living and working with different kinds of people, and I learned about religions and philosophies other than my own from a group of outstanding scholars.

Each summer I shared my assignments with students from all over the world. The first year I worked in a mental hospital, a project that was consistent with my premedical interest. Another year, I worked with a small group of students out of Waterbury, Vermont, in a peace caravan. I learned to serve the poor during those summers. While I was expanding my mind, I also was learning how to be a missionary in my own country.

Following high school graduation, I enrolled in Johnson C. Smith University, a historically black college in Charlotte, North Carolina. After graduating with a major in biology, I taught school. Later, I went to graduate school and completed a master's degree. My plan to become a medical missionary was derailed when I met and fell in love with Theaoseus while in college. He had come from a farm family and wanted to become a lawyer. He did become a lawyer, and we have been married for more than forty years and are the parents of four children and grandparents of five grandchildren.

Once I became a mother, I began to focus on the community around me. It's a natural evolution for most of us: when we take on the responsibility of raising our children, we want our community to be the best place for them to grow up.

The Disappearance of the African American Farmer

Long before I came to Congress, I worked to improve the lives and opportunities of the rural poor as a volunteer and as a county commissioner. When I arrived in the House of Representatives in 1993, I sought appointment to the Agriculture Committee because I knew it would provide an excellent opportunity for me to improve the quality of life for my constituents. The First Congressional District of North Carolina, which I represent, is largely rural and poor, and I am always cognizant of the needs of the underprivileged.

My district is located in the eastern part of North Carolina, an area that for the most part is economically disadvantaged. It contains a large number of farms, big and small in terms of acreage and production. I am disturbed by the continuous loss of small farms, particularly those owned by African Americans. I am outraged that part of the problem is the result of discriminatory practices by agents of our government against minority farmers seeking loans. These issues rarely make headlines even though farmers, especially small family farmers and ranchers, are vital to America's future. Although conventional wisdom leads people to believe that race discrimination in lending is a thing of the past, it is not!

In 1959, America had more than 2.4 million small farms, that is, those with fewer than 180 acres. By 1992, the number of small farms had declined to 1.1 million. But the number of African American farmers nationally dwindled to only 1 percent, at a rate three times that of white farmers. In my own state of North Carolina, the percentage of minority farmers declined by 64 percent between 1978 and 1992.

In 1990, almost a quarter of all farm households had incomes below the poverty line. That was more than twice the national average. Of course, there are many reasons for the decline in small farms, among them globalization of commerce with worldwide markets, economies of scale, limited access to capital, and technological advances. All of these pressures gathered to create an extraordinary impact on minority farmers and ranchers.

But there is more to the story than all the standard reasons for why so many small farms have disappeared. Over and over again, local representatives of the U.S. Department of Agriculture (USDA), which was established to assist small farmers and ranchers, have engaged in well-documented incidents of discrimination in extending credit to minority farmers.

The issue was first raised in 1965, when the U.S. Commission on Civil Rights reported that the USDA discriminated against minority farmers. In 1997, thirty-two years later, another government study came to the identical conclusion.

The 1997 study was conducted by a task force of top USDA officials who traveled the nation to investigate complaints of discrimination. The group interviewed USDA employees, who described racial animosity and sex discrimination in many of the department's 2,500 local offices.

Minority farmers complained to the task force that their numbers have diminished at the hands of local officials, who not only subject them to credit standards different from white applicants' but also delay and then deny loan applications. Some minority farmers charged the USDA with conspiring to foreclose on their land. *I wonder if these officials ever considered what it means for a farmer to lose everything?*

The task force documented decades of discrimination against minorities and women in the USDA and proposed ninety-two recommendations for change. As a result, I introduced H.R. 2185, the USDA Accountability and Equity Act, to implement those recommendations that require legislation. Among other things, I want to ensure that county committees will not discriminate against any employee or any applicant for a loan because of race or gender. My legislation requires the local committees to be composed of a representative, diverse group of citizens.

For far too long, the issue of the disappearance of minority farmers has gone unnoticed at the highest levels of our government. In December 1997, I succeeded in organizing a meeting of small farmers with President Bill Clinton to address the issue of access to credit for small farmers as well as more than one thousand long-standing, unresolved discrimination complaints against the USDA.

I have been frustrated and disappointed that justice has been delayed for so many people for so long and hope my intervention will make a difference.

Feeding the Hungry

I think it is time to stop picking on poor people. Our nation's strength is not the result of advanced technology, its economic base, or military might. The real strength of America is in its compassion for people, those who live in the shadows of life, those who are hungry.

I continue to be an advocate of extending food stamps and the Women's, Infants, and Children's (WIC) program. There is no excuse for us to have hungry people in a nation whose farmers provide more than enough food and fiber to meet the needs of all Americans as well as many nations overseas.

Less than 3 percent of the entire federal budget is targeted for feeding the hungry. But in fighting hunger we are in the midst of a struggle that will influence American lives for many generations because it affects the future of so many children.

In 1996, many of us agreed that our welfare system needed to be reformed, and we were right to do so—but reform should move people out of poverty, not into poverty. The 1996 welfare reform act permits "able bodied" adults to receive food stamps for no more than three months in any thirty-six-month period. Most legal immigrants once eligible for food stamps are no longer eligible.

Nutrition programs are essential to the well-being of millions of citizens—the disadvantaged, children, the elderly, and the disabled. These are people who often cannot provide for themselves. They aren't asking for very much; just a little food to help get through the day, keep their children alert in school, or assist adults in being productive on the job or in searching for a job. In many cases nutrition programs provide the only decent daily food for millions of the nation's poor.

Perhaps those of us who want to deny people the chance to eat or feed their families do so because we do not see them. We do not know them. And because we don't see or know them, we have an image of them that is false.

Many of America's twenty-five million food stamp recipients have jobs and still cannot afford to feed their families adequately. I am concerned that in our zeal to balance the federal budget, we are failing to balance our priorities, forcing many of our citizens to slide rapidly toward the bottom of society.

My concern for the poor, especially children, is shared by colleagues on both sides of the aisle. As a result, I have worked with Republicans and Democrats on legislation extending food stamp benefits to those who are seeking work and cannot find it, including eligible legal immigrants.

We also want to ensure that the WIC program is adequately funded, because it works. Historically, every dollar spent on WIC has saved at least three dollars in health care costs. My goal is to eliminate hunger as a way of life for people. There is a cure for hunger, and Congress has the remedy.

Collective Action

We need advocates on the outside to help those of us inside Congress continue the fight to feed people, and to rekindle the generous spirit of Americans in helping the poor. I tell volunteers in the antihunger movement that they are an active house of worship. Unlike others, they don't sit in comfortable pews, shielded by stained glass windows, protected from people they don't want to see. They are willing to go out and help those citizens who are "invisible" to others. When advocates help make visible the struggles of people who are otherwise invisible, it strengthens the ability of policymakers like me to make change.

As a woman in politics, I understand the value of collective action. I learned it as a young mother working with others to ensure a community that was safe and healthy for everyone's children in order to protect my own children. I learned it in my summers with the AFSC helping people less fortunate than me. I learned it from the examples of Sojourner Truth, Harriet Tubman, Mary McLeod Bethune, and Rosa Parks. Like most committed women, and like me, they were women of faith.

These are challenging times that will test our faith again and again as we fight threats to the progress we have made in this nation since my childhood in the 1940s and 1950s. We must protect our children, grandchildren, the elderly, and our own communities by restoring America's sense of responsibility to the less fortunate in society.

Women historically have viewed the family as community and the community as family. It's important for the neighborhood to be decent for everyone's kids if we are to meet our primary responsibility of protecting and nurturing our own kids. A commitment to the community by mothers stems from a desire to enhance and enrich opportunities for their own families.

Women who work collectively to solve problems come to understand that each of us has strengths and each has weaknesses. We gain comfort and courage by recognizing that we can lean on one another when we are tired and inspire each other when we are fresh.

Together we can make progress, even if sometimes it appears to be beyond our reach. Progress is just ahead at the land's horizon. I often contemplate the horizon, as both a place and a symbol. The horizon, of course, is a matter of geography—where the trees meet the sky. But it is also a way to think about what is next, what is in the future, and how we will progress.

As a member of Congress I look at the horizon from two perspectives: from Washington and from my home in North Carolina. From both places, from either view, despite the problems, the horizon looks promising. I see progress ahead.

THE MEASURE OF WOMAN

KATHLEEN KENNEDY TOWNSEND was elected in 1994 as Maryland's first woman lieutenant governor. She chairs the state's Cabinet Council on Criminal and Juvenile Justice and the Systems Reform Task Force for Children and Youth, and co-chairs the Maryland Family Violence Council. Prior to her election Townsend was deputy assistant attorney general in the U.S. Department of Justice. She has taught at the University of Pennsylvania, the University of Maryland-Baltimore County, and at Essex and Dundalk Community Colleges. She was the first executive director of the Maryland Student Service Alliance, which she founded to inspire young people to serve their communities. She serves on the boards of the National Institute for Women's Policy Research and of Radcliffe College. She holds a B.A. degree from Harvard University and a J.D. degree from New Mexico School of Law.

The Measure of Woman

KATHLEEN KENNEDY TOWNSEND

A S THE CENTURY that saw the dawn of the women's movement draws to a close, one thing is clear. The traditional expectations of women, to a large extent, have been smashed. The challenge to women today is to replace those expectations with new ones that allow a woman to realize her fullest potential and contribute in a meaningful way to her family, community, and country.

We used to know what was the measure of a woman. Our society judged a woman most directly on her home life: Her home, her husband, her children. We judged a woman on her loyalty to those three pillars of her life. In essence, we measured her by the extent to which she sacrificed herself for those around her.

In many ways those days are gone. No one can mistake the contributions of women to the political, economic, and cultural life of our country and our world. With each generation, our daughters are offered more and greater examples of the possibilities that lie before them. Today, perhaps for the first time in history, we may honestly say to our daughters that no door is shut to them, that there are no artificial limits on the possibility for individual achievement.

But in concentrating on ourselves, something has been lacking. Many women who have focused on the traditional, that is to say, male, areas of achievement, such as business, law, and finance, have found that world unsatisfying and unfulfilling. Many women, reacting to the traditional limits and expectations about their roles, have sacrificed values that have long made women's lives most satisfying: values that emphasized their children, their families, and their communities.

Women are now coming full circle. We have lived with our ambition stifled and found it intolerable—but we are finding aggressive individualism to be weak and deficient as well. Without abandoning altogether the drive for personal achievement, many women are rediscovering the fulfillment that comes from working not merely for ourselves. Paradoxically, our individual lives are most fulfilled when we are willing to serve something greater than ourselves.

The Habit of Service

The threads of service run deep throughout my life. My family has always been involved in the service of our community or country. My great-grandfather was a ward boss and Massachusetts state senator. My grandfather served as an ambassador and the chairman of the Securities and Exchange Commission. My father and my uncle John both were decorated for their service in World War II. My uncle Joseph gave his life in that war. The memory of his sacrifice for the noblest cause, freedom, still inspires my family.

Many of my earliest memories are of being taught about my obligation to serve our country. America had been very good to the

Kennedys; we had an obligation to repay the good fortune we found here.

I remember the time my father returned from a trip to the Mississippi Delta, which he toured to understand better the nature of the problems of poverty and race relations. He returned to our large house in the rolling Virginia hills, entered our nicely set dining room with its pressed linen, fine china, and crystal chandeliers, and said, "A whole family lives in a shack the size of this dining room. The children's tummies stick out because they have no food and are covered in sores. Do you know how lucky you are? Do you *know* how *lucky* you are? Do something for your country."

There is only so much a young girl can do, but it seems that I was always involved in something. As a child I visited senior centers, collected cans of food for the hungry, and volunteered in my Aunt Eunice's camp for the retarded (which eventually developed into the Special Olympics).

Religion, which was at least as strong an influence in our lives as politics, offered the same lessons of service. I spent most of my childhood in Catholic school classrooms presided over by nuns, who served as outstanding role models. Here were women who gave up everything—material possessions, family, and careers—because they felt a call to serve their communities and their God. They chose to forego all the pursuits that we thought might make us happy, yet they carried themselves with a serene satisfaction and contentment that could come only from a life well-lived.

They taught us, over and over again, St. Luke's admonition that from those to whom much is given, much is expected. Each class adopted a missionary. My best friend Anne Coffey's uncle was a missionary priest in Chol-Chol, Chile, so naturally we adopted Father Jurg Mundell. We prayed for him, and sent money that we collected. In turn, he sent pictures and wrote letters describing life in a small village. We felt connected to this far-away missionary and to the idea that each of us, too, should take risks to do good.

Works of charity do not always come easily to young children, but the nuns' examples, and the expectation that we also would make giving a regular part of our life, washed away many of the second thoughts and rationalizations. Always, the focus was less on what giving did for us, the givers, and more on what it did for those who needed our help.

When I was twelve years old, for instance, a friend and I delivered a Christmas dinner to a family in a tenement building in inner-city Washington. We walked up three flights of narrow, poorly lit stairs to deliver turkey, stuffing, vegetables, and a bag of toys. After a little boy greeted us at the door, his mother quickly came, thanked us, took the packages—and then we left.

The entire exchange took less than five minutes. I still recall the vaguely embarrassed feeling I had as I walked down the stairs. Were they resentful of our good fortune? Had we made the mother feel inadequate because she had *not* provided for her children?

Those were good questions but ones that also could be enlisted to rationalize not making further trips into the ghetto. Although it is easy to dismiss the trip as just another manifestation of the patronizing and insincere Lady Bountiful, the bottom line is that there was a good result. The family had a real Christmas dinner.

As uniform as the message was to serve, how it manifested itself in my family was split along gender lines. The men held cabinet posts, ran for the Senate, or for president. The women took care of children and were engaged in volunteer work, like my aunt Eunice's work for the mentally retarded.

If happiness is, as the Greeks defined it, using one's talents along the lines of excellence, then limiting the opportunities for a woman's self-expression to her clothes, her home, and the parties she throws is a recipe for depression and anxiety. It is telling that my grandmother Rose would often tell me stories about how her father had not let her go to Wellesley College as she had wished. This regret was disclosed by a woman who presided—with unequaled dignity—over one of the most accomplished political families in American history!

Yet she wanted something for herself, an accomplishment she could call her own.

As I left high school for college, the vague outlines of a good life began to take shape. I could never leave behind the habit of service—it was too deeply rooted in my life. But at eighteen, I was being afforded an opportunity my grandmother was not: a first-class education, and with it, the tools and the opportunity to make a difference in the nation and the world. The stage was bigger, the spectrum of possibilities more brilliant, yet the pulse of service would always beat underneath.

Paradoxes of the Women's Movement

Harvard University offered a perfect vantage point from which to watch and participate in the embryonic women's movement. Slowly but ineluctably, women were moving in circles once closed to us. More role models were presented to us, both from the past (Susan B. Anthony and the early suffragists) and the present (Gloria Steinem and Betty Friedan, for instance).

We faced a quandary, however. The Vietnam War and the civil rights movement showed clearly the deep flaws in the world men had created. It was cold, violent, and cruel, everything the private worlds women had created in their homes and in their volunteer work were not. The "system," as it appeared to us, was corrupt. How could we justify pursuing the traditional routes of ambitious people: politics, law, medicine, or business? It was a puzzle faced by the young women and men of my class alike. Fewer graduates from my class went on to Harvard business school than any other class in history. We wanted to change the world, not change ourselves to fit into it.

For this reason, the first two decades of the women's movement were unsettling for me. Many feminists had insisted that women should succeed in traditional roles—lawyers, doctors, businesspersons. I recall an advertisement in *Ms.* magazine that showed a suited woman sitting in a board room.

Under the very worthy guise of casting off Paleolithic attitudes toward women and femininity, many women merely tried to imitate men and ended up copying their worst attribute, namely, the prizing of individual achievement over common progress. The National Organization for Women went on record to oppose volunteering by women in fields such as health care and social work because it was "exploitive" and reinforced traditional sex roles.

I remember a conversation I had with an older friend of mine in the early 1980s. She noticed an enormous change in women's attitudes. "I can hardly get anyone to help me now," she complains. "They are either out making money, or if I do find someone willing to help, she wants to get paid as a consultant." When I asked another friend about voluntarism, she quickly replied, "I think it's terrible. I want to get *paid* for what I do. I want people to value it. And money is the only way anybody will think it's important."

The Legacy of the Women's Movement

The long-standing exclusion of women from all but a few professions was wrong and self-defeating for all of us. Yet many women's search for equal opportunity led them to denigrate such traditional pursuits as family and volunteering. This was doubly tragic because the unthinking pursuit of money and respectability—until recently, largely a male obsession—has sapped the nation's strength. It has led many of our most talented people into vocations of little or no use for the rest of us and fostered selfishness and narcissism.

Whenever possible, women and men should try to do what satisfies them most. This not only means that women should continue to volunteer; perhaps more important, it means that men should volunteer much more. Rather than reject voluntarism, women should see its revival as an opportunity for leadership in areas in which they've long excelled—not just caring for family but caring for others as well.

In its progression the women's movement has an opportunity to liberate men as well. If men see women dissatisfied with a purely self-oriented life and going out of their way to spend more time with their families, perhaps it will rub off on them. Perhaps many men can also learn that the tunnel vision of a career-first life falls far short. The values with which we women have conducted our private lives—compassion, generosity, and magnanimity—are now introduced to the public world. If we work for it, these values can take root and grow into every sphere of society. The values of women can become the values of our nation.

In the end this may be the enduring legacy of the women's movement and its most profound contribution to the country. The spirit of service that women have traditionally brought to family and community can now be expressed on a broader scale and therefore have a greater impact.

The most obvious example of how this is playing out is through politics. Given my family background, it should come to no one's surprise that this is where I have sought to make my mark. I've become the first woman lieutenant governor of Maryland and the first woman in my family to hold public office. Like many other women politicians, I've focused much of my energy on topics and initiatives that have been neglected in years past.

For instance, I organized the effort to institute the first statewide community service graduation requirement for high school students. I started the first statewide character education office to help children learn right from wrong, as well as fact from fiction. I have redirected the state's domestic violence and anticrime strategy to give it a more comprehensive, community-oriented foundation. In each instance, I have tried to combine the best traditions of women's historical commitment to community with the high expectations and ambitions of the women's movement.

I am not alone. Over the past twenty-five years, the percentages of women holding office at the local, state, and federal level have all more than doubled. Although there is not yet full parity, 50 percent representation, the steady and unbroken march of progress suggests that the day is not far off. Every ceiling that is shattered, such as Madeleine Albright's ascent to the office of secretary of state, inspires more women to pursue the spectrum of possibilities that lies before them.

At the same time, women are making a mark by serving as advocates. Marian Wright Edelman of the Children's Defense Fund, Sarah Brady, author of the Brady Law to regulate handgun purchases, and Elizabeth Dole of the American Red Cross are showing that elected office is not the only way for women to make a difference in politics.

What this adds up to is nothing less than the resurrection and revitalization of the most important principles underlying the American experiment: a check on individualism's darker side with the spirit of community.

The current of individual liberty and the extraordinary openness of American life and opportunity has been perhaps our greatest contribution to the world. It has beaten all restraints of custom, government, tradition; it has swept away the old and established, in science and business, education and agriculture, medicine and war. No serious person would propose to change or limit that freedom of individual life and effort. It is, in any event, firmly enshrined in the United States Constitution itself.

But there is a darker side. Individualism unchecked can seem sometimes like an infection run wild. The business enterprise that gives life to a community is later discovered to have poisoned it with pollution. The freedom of expression that shields the artist and the dissenter also shields the most repellent pornographer.

Deeper even than this dark side is the fundamental problem, the tension of any commercial society. Commerce creates wealth, raises living standards, supports the advancement of civilization. Yet for whole periods of our history, commerce has seemed to immerse the whole nation in greed, rapaciousness, dishonesty, and the exaltation of money and to contribute to the death or burial of virtue.

In the last analysis, all nations depend for their survival on the existence of virtues that have nothing to do with money. Courage, self-sacrifice, honor, duty, and truth: these are the essential virtues of a republic, and none of them can be bought. But they can be encouraged, nurtured, and strengthened. They stem from an understanding that there are principles and causes worth fighting for, worth sacrificing for. The measure of a woman today is determined by the extent to which she applies the values we cherished and celebrated throughout history, the values that women have always represented, to the range of new opportunities that lie before us all. If we look at our past with clear eyes and restore those immutable and intrinsic values, we can remake the world.

CAROL MOSELEY-BRAUN, United States senator (Democrat, Illinois), is the first African American woman elected to the U.S. Senate and the first to represent Illinois in that position. From 1979 to 1988, she served as a member and floor leader of the Illinois state legislature. She was the elected Cook County recorder of deeds from 1988 to 1992 and was an assistant United States attorney from 1973 to 1997. She is the first woman permanent member of the Senate Finance Committee and serves on the Banking, Housing, and Urban Affairs Committee and the Special Committee on Aging. Moseley-Braun is a former member of the Judiciary Committee, the Small Business Committee, and the Bipartisan Commission on Entitlement and Tax Reform. She holds a B.A. degree from the University of Illinois at Chicago and a J.D. degree from the University of Chicago Law School.

Standing Alone

CAROL MOSELEY-BRAUN

People often ask me what it is like to be the first and only African American woman ever elected to the United States Senate. I must admit that when I first arrived, some of my Senate colleagues were plainly surprised to see me. The idea that an African American woman might be elected to that very exclusive club had simply not occurred to them.

I did not just fall out of the sky and into the Senate. I have been involved in politics for a long time. I spent ten years in the Illinois state legislature and three years as recorder of deeds in Cook County.

My first election to the legislature was in 1978. After two terms I was chosen as the first woman assistant majority leader to serve in the Illinois House of Representatives. When I was elected Cook County recorder of deeds in 1988, I became the first woman and first black person to hold countywide executive office.

Because of who I am and when I was born, I have repeatedly had the experience of being the first black person to do this or the first woman to do that. Over the years I have learned to take a deep breath—and then get to work. That's what I did when I first arrived in the United States Senate.

I think of public service as a form of patriotism. By definition, *patriotism* means giving of oneself to the benefit and the good of one's country. We have gotten away from using the word *patriotism*, perhaps because it is at once so profound and so quaint. But it is important to remind ourselves that when we work for the improvement of our society, we work for the preservation of our country. By undertaking that task, women and leaders of color are patriots.

Our Legacy

Each of us carries on a brilliant tradition, each takes up the challenge of living up to the legacy of our ancestors while giving our children no less than we have inherited. All of us, by our service to community and country, follow and breathe life into that noble tradition. The difficult challenges of our time are made no less difficult by our unity and our vision.

Mary McLeod Bethune once spoke to that vision in her famous "Last Will and Testament" (as outlined by Rackham Holt in his 1964 biography *Mary McLeod Bethune*): "Here, then is my legacy: I leave you love. . . . I leave you hope. . . . I leave you a thirst for education. . . . I leave you faith. . . . I leave you racial dignity. . . . I leave you a desire to live harmoniously with your fellow men. . . . I leave you finally a responsibility to our young people."

That legacy is with us. We are called upon to draw on the strength, the example, and the vision of Mary McLeod Bethune, Sojourner Truth, Rosa Parks, and all those who helped bring us this far.

What their stories of struggle tell us, most importantly, is that progress is not linear. Instead, it takes twists and turns, detours and sidetracks. It surprises and disappoints us. Just when we thought some great evil has been conquered, another version of it crops up wearing a new guise, and we are called upon to fight it once again.

But fight it we must. The legacy of the struggle and the critical, heart-wrenching duty to make that struggle count in the lives of the next generation demand no less.

Entering the Senate

I will never forget my first official meeting as a United States senator. Our organizational meeting was held in the old Senate chamber in the Capitol building, which has not been used for the regular business of the Senate since the 1850s. I sought out the chair of the senator from Illinois who last served in the old chamber.

There, in the third row, I found the seat held by Illinois senator Stephen Douglas, who served in the Senate from 1846 until his death in 1861. Douglas was the senator who proposed the divisive Kansas-Nebraska Act in 1854, allowing settlers in the territories of our westward-expanding nation to vote on whether to enter the union as slave states or free states. The bill helped sink the Whig Party. It also gave birth the same year to the Republican Party, which demanded that slavery be excluded from the territories.

When Douglas served, there were not any people of color in the Senate, or any women, as neither were then considered full citizens of this country—the words and promises of the Declaration of Independence and the Constitution notwithstanding.

In 1858, when Douglas ran for reelection, his opponent was Abraham Lincoln, who challenged him in what are known as the

Lincoln-Douglas debates. Lincoln won the debates, but Douglas won the election, and so became the senator from Illinois once again. Two years later, Lincoln defeated Douglas in the presidential election and led this country through the most painful chapter of its history—the great Civil War.

Following the Civil War, two men of African descent became senators, Hiram Revels and Blanche K. Bruce. Their tenure in the Senate was marked by hostility and resistance in their home state of Mississippi during that appalling period of our history known as the Reconstruction. When the Reconstruction was over, the Senate would not see another American of African descent until Edward Brooke of Massachusetts, who served from 1967 to 1976.

The people of Illinois, over two million of them, chose to integrate the United States Senate with my election in 1992. When I sat in the seat once occupied by Stephen Douglas, I could not help but think of the struggle and sacrifice of all those who had fought for freedom. Standing on the shoulders of those giants, I was able to come to the Senate and take Douglas's seat. But the progress was not linear.

An Inclusive Democracy

The progress and the victory are not mine, however. The progress lies in the opening up of our democracy to voices and perspectives that might not otherwise be heard. It should be self-evident, but unfortunately is not, that the more inclusive our democratic institutions (as well as our social and economic ones), the better those institutions are able to address and resolve the concerns of all of the people.

A society that taps the talent of 100 percent of its people is a stronger society, because it can draw on a broader talent pool. A community that gives all of its members a chance to contribute to the maximum extent of their ability is a stronger community, because it benefits from a broader contribution.

The opening up of the process to all Americans makes our democracy work more efficiently because governance becomes reflective, as well as representative, of all of the people. For example, having a woman of color in the room of the Senate Finance Committee matters when issues touching on taxes, retirement security, and child care are raised.

The issue of affirmative action, and the impending attempt to expand nationally California's Proposition 209 abolishing affirmative action, is a poignant example of the twists and turns that progress can, and does, take. The great moral victory of the civil rights movement set the stage for an effort to take on, and resolve, the societal and economic distortions that two hundred years of slavery and segregation had created for our country.

The death of Jim Crow left us with a country still divided into two societies, one black and one white. A generation took up the challenge, not of paying reparations to the Americans who had been so disenfranchised but of providing enhanced opportunities and a chance to catch up. That generation offered affirmative action as a structural response to a structural distortion of our society.

A class of Americans of African descent developed and began to integrate our nation socially and economically. A class of women entrepreneurs began to emerge, aided by this structural response to the distortion that had kept women out of the public sphere. Affirmative action worked in education, the professions, and the marketplace.

A New Civil Rights Struggle

But the successes of affirmative action ran into the short memories of those who were happy to forget history and to ignore the reality that racism and sexism did not die with Jim Crow. Fairness is a fundamental American value; so is the notion of individual merit. The supporters of Proposition 209 succeeded in convincing a majority of Californians that efforts to cure a long-standing structural distortion in our society were unfair to individuals who were not themselves the architects of the structure.

The obvious reality is that our society is constructed on the traditional station of women and minorities. Inasmuch as that traditional station relies on unfairness and inequality, American leaders must assume the challenge to change it.

Women do not earn 75 percent of the earnings of men in the same jobs because they are 25 percent less competent or pay 25 percent less for food. It should come as no surprise, further, that this gender gap in earnings carries over into retirement, and therefore 80 percent of the elderly poor are women. Americans of African descent remain proportionately poorer, sicker, more imprisoned, less educated, not because of accident, but because of the distortions created in today's society by institutional structures crafted over time.

The resolution and reform of these structural distortions in our society is an important undertaking not just for the individuals who would personally benefit, but for communities, society, and the country as a whole. America is never so magnificent as when it reflects its nobler traditions. Justice and equality and opportunity based on capacity and merit are among the defining values of our country. I am committed to communicating those values in ways the majority community can understand and embrace.

How many times have you heard the statement: "I have never had any slaves, I am not a racist, and it is not fair that someone should have a leg up on me because that person is black"? I think such arguments fail to recognize that the issue is not one of unfairness to any person but of fairness to our country. How long can America bear the weight of a segregated society? What costs are borne by all of us because of the deficits Jim Crow left? Is any competition defined by the privilege associated with white supremacy ever fair?

The battleground for affirmative action represents the new frontier of the civil rights struggle for the complete integration of people of color and women into American society. We have watched the fallout over minority recruitment in California's system of higher education since passage of Proposition 209. It confirms that the elimination of affirmative action creates a setback in the progress of integration. We are witnessing a retrenchment, and it is a frightening prospect for America.

A True Meritocracy

The real challenge lies in capturing the hearts and minds of the people when we address the issues of race and gender in contemporary society. It will take people of good will of all races, men and women, to create the climate of opinion, the expectation, that America can and must shape policy responses that will move us forward, not backward, toward integrating all its people into a true American meritocracy. Racism and sexism must be confronted honestly, with the understanding that the future of our country is at stake.

The past really is prologue in that regard. Most white Americans do not see themselves as racist, nor would they support discrimination against people of color. Similarly, most men don't see themselves as sexist. That racism is no longer overt or popular is a great victory. Today the expectations of the American people are that we should have a color-blind society and that nondiscrimination must be a universally held value. Now we are called upon to celebrate and build upon those expectations, as we make the case that the goal of equality of opportunity is achieved when every

American makes a commitment to resolving the distortions that we have yet to overcome.

To those who oppose affirmative action, the question must be asked: What have you done to undo the privileges of the past? How have you contributed to the end of racism? What ideas can you contribute for reconciling America to all its people? What steps have you taken to open the doors of opportunity?

Each person makes a difference in shaping the climate of opinion from which policy will emerge. Each of us has a role to play in directing the course our country will take. Our challenge is to reach outside of our private lives to shape our community.

All individuals have a role and a duty to use the resources at their personal disposal to serve the public interest. In meeting that challenge, we will make the world our children inherit a more just society and one in which talent and ability, not color or gender or station, will determine their path.

I am most encouraged by a conversation I had with a little girl in a grammar school classroom after my election to the Senate. I had given a speech in which I bragged about the fact that eight women were then serving in the Senate—a historic high water mark. When I finished, the little girl raised her hand and asked in an inquisitive voice: "Eight women out of one hundred senators? Is that all?" Her expectation was that the proportion of women in the Senate would be the same as the proportion of girls in her classroom. Her expectation was one of equality.

We Americans have inherited an expectation of freedom. As the twentieth century comes to an end, it is our responsibility to endow the next generation with a legacy of equality. Dr. Martin Luther King once said, "The arc of the moral universe is long, but it bends toward justice." We must never forget that in fighting for equality we are waging a war for justice. As we define an America that draws deeply on the strengths of all its people, we will purge the impulse to oppress any of its citizens.

Mary McLeod Bethune would be very proud of her daughters. By our vision we are ensuring that America lives up to her promise. By our activism we are forcing America to reach her potential. By our patriotism we will make America exceed her wildest dreams.

I am determined to make a difference.

SARAH BRADY became the chair of Handgun Control, Inc. (HCI) in 1989. She also chairs the Center to Prevent Handgun Violence, which works to reduce gun violence through education, research, and legal advocacy. A graduate of William and Mary College, she was a public school teacher in Virginia from 1964 to 1968. From 1968 to 1970, she was assistant to the campaign director at the National Republican Congressional Committee. In 1970, she joined the staff of Representative Mike McKevitt (Republican, Colorado) and from 1971 to 1974 worked for Representative Joseph J. Maraziti (Republican, New Jersey). During the next four years she was director of administration and coordinator of field services for the Republican National Committee. A winner of many awards, Brady was named a 1997 Frontrunner by the Sara Lee Foundation, and in 1993 received the Leadership Award of the League of Women Voters.

Battling for My Cause

SARAH BRADY

W HEN I MARRIED Jim Brady in 1973 and we set out on our life
together, I never imagined I would be in the place I am now.
By March 30, 1981, our life was perfect. Everything was on track.
We had an adorable son named Scott who had just turned two years
old. Jim had been appointed to his ideal job: White House press secretary to newly elected President Ronald Reagan. All of our dreams
had come true.

In an instant our lives changed forever. On a rainy Monday afternoon in front of the Washington Hilton Hotel, our dreams were
shattered by John Hinckley's assassination attempt on President Reagan. President Reagan was shot and so was Jim. We almost lost the
president of the United States, and we almost lost Jim.

I have always loved politics and campaigns. Both my mother and
father were interested in government and politics and always kept us

informed about the latest news, especially since we lived next door to the nation's capital, in Alexandria, Virginia.

After I graduated from William and Mary College in 1964, I taught in public schools for four years. I might have selected a different career, but in those days, teaching and nursing were the most common options for a woman. Everything in my world changed when my brother was drafted to fight in the Vietnam War, and something in me snapped. I guess I grew up.

I got involved in civil rights and other serious issues and went to work for the National Republican Campaign Committee. It was in that job that I was first introduced to Jim Brady. Some people thought he was after my money—campaign money, that is—because it was my office that provided money to Republican congressional candidates. Jim was seeking money for a congressional candidate from Illinois. I can't even remember whether the candidate got the money, but Jim did win my heart.

From 1970 to 1974 I worked in two congressional offices and then went to work for the Republican National Committee (RNC). I had always had different plans for myself once I married: I envisioned myself as a stay-at-home mom and wife. When Scott was born, I resigned from the RNC.

My traditional and, in my eyes, idyllic existence didn't last very long. On March 30, 1981, I was watching television and Scott was playing when a news bulletin interrupted the program to announce that President Reagan had been shot. I had no idea that Jim had also been shot until the phone rang and I got the news.

I rushed to the hospital to be with Jim. Only later did I discover that the three major television networks had reported his death. Miraculously, Jim survived, thanks to the heroism of the Secret Service, a skilled medical team, and Jim's own determination. After several long months of rehabilitation and many disheartening setbacks, Jim finally came home. The left side of his body was paralyzed and his speech was impaired.

Suddenly I became the provider and decision maker for both my husband and my young son. For the next several years I focused all of my energy on taking care of Jim and our son, Scott, and keeping our family together.

A Close Call

Most people assume it was Jim's wounding in Hinckley's assassination attempt on President Reagan that motivated me to get involved in gun control. It was, however, an incident in 1985 involving our son that truly pushed me into action.

One day while we were visiting family in Jim's hometown of Centralia, Illinois, Scott and I decided to go swimming with some friends. We climbed into our friend's pickup truck, where Scott found a gun on the seat. Thinking it was a toy, he began playing with it. I told him never to point a gun, even a toy, at a person and took it away from him. I was shocked to discover that the gun was real and it was loaded. It was a .22 caliber "Saturday night special," a crummy little gun just like the one John Hinckley used to shoot my husband.

In a matter of seconds a gun almost brought another tragedy to our family. Fortunately, neither of us was hurt. I wondered what kind of world we lived in where five-year-olds and mentally unstable people like John Hinckley could so easily get their hands on guns. I was furious! I decided to do whatever I could to prevent other families from experiencing the same tragedy that we had.

When we returned home, I heard on the news that the National Rifle Association (NRA) was working to rescind the 1968 Gun Control Act. I picked up the phone and called the NRA. It was about 7:30 at night, so whoever answered the phone probably was on the cleaning crew. I didn't care—I was so mad, I told the voice on the other end, "You don't know me, but my name is Sarah Brady, and I am going to do everything I can to put the NRA out of business." Then I called Handgun Control, Inc. (HCI), and volunteered to help. I've been at it ever since. I started out by writing letters, lobbying, and testifying before Congress. In 1989, I was elected chair of HCI, a position I still hold today.

At HCI, our goal is not to ban guns, but simply to keep handguns out of the hands of criminals and children. I grew up with guns and learned gun safety from my father, who was an FBI agent. Guns were part of my family's life because they were part of my father's life. When he came home from work every day wearing his business suit, he went right to his room, changed clothes, and locked away his gun—all before saying, "Hi, honey I'm home." My father never considered himself "home" until he made sure that gun was safely locked away.

My father always carried a service revolver to work. He also had hunted in his youth. But he used to complain that Americans are much too casual about guns. Not only was his service weapon always under lock and key in our house, he also never even let me look at it. It was a practice that made sense then and still makes sense today.

Jim's wounding was not my first brush with gun violence. When I was a teenager, someone shot a bullet in my car window. The police said it was probably a young person who was playing with a gun—probably just a random shot with no malice intended. I don't think I gave it much thought until many years later when a much more serious shooting totally changed my life.

Our Proudest Moment

When I first became involved with Handgun Control, we were fighting for legislation that would require a waiting period and a background check for every purchaser of a handgun. The idea was simple:

to establish a "cooling off" period and give police time to conduct a background check on the potential purchaser.

Our country already had established several categories of "prohibited purchasers," including convicted felons, juveniles, people judged as mentally ill by the courts, and fugitives from justice. At the time, at least thirty-two states did not require a waiting period or a background check, relying instead on a ludicrous honor system that meant anyone trying to buy a gun could lie about his or her past and not get caught.

In 1987, the legislation designed to close this loophole was first introduced in Congress and became known as the Brady bill, named for my husband. It was endorsed by every major law enforcement organization as well as former Presidents Reagan, Carter, Ford, and Nixon. Public opinion surveys revealed that nine out of ten Americans supported the Brady bill.

Even so, the Brady bill was defeated in the House of Representatives in September 1988, thanks to the well-financed efforts of the gun lobby. Opponents of the Brady bill argued that a waiting period was "inconvenient." In the Brady household, we could tell them something about inconvenience: the pain, the injuries, and the cost—emotional and financial—that can result from a gunshot wound.

For five more years we lobbied to pass the Brady bill. At times we thought it would never even be scheduled by the House leadership for a full debate and vote. Finally, in 1991 it passed both houses of Congress. But opponents killed the bill in conference committee by threatening a filibuster, and President Bush promised to veto the Brady bill if it reached his desk.

In 1993, after he was elected president, Bill Clinton promised in his State of the Union address to sign the Brady bill if Congress passed it. Once again we went through many moments of thinking the bill was going to be filibustered to death. Thanks to public support, the efforts of law enforcement, and the effective work of HCI and other organizations supporting our position, it finally passed. It had taken seven long years. President Clinton kept his promise and signed the Brady bill into law in November 1993, to take effect on February 28, 1994.

It was the proudest moment of our lives.

Gun Laws Work

The gun lobby likes to argue that gun laws penalize only law-abiding citizens and that the laws don't work. They are wrong. In the first four years of the Brady Act, background checks nationwide stopped approximately 173,000 convicted felons and other prohibited purchasers from buying handguns. According to data analyzed from the FBI Uniform Crime Report, the percentage of violent crimes committed with firearms has declined dramatically—even more dramatically than the overall rate of decline in violent crime. Department of Justice data show that the Brady Law also has reduced the number of guns trafficked from states with lax gun laws to those with stricter laws, thereby reducing the number of illegal guns on the streets.

The number of federally licensed firearms dealers (FFLs) has also declined. Before the Brady Law, the licenses, which allow people to buy guns wholesale and resell them for a profit, were cheap and easy to acquire. The Bureau of Alcohol, Tobacco and Firearms (ATF) did not have the resources to ensure that every FFL was operating a legitimate business. As a result, unscrupulous FFLs became a primary source of illegal guns; some sold guns out of the trunks of cars and on street corners. Because of the increased cost of licenses, required background checks of dealers, and intensified supervision by the ATF, FFLs have declined by more than 50 percent.

In 1994, we scored another victory with passage of the assault weapons ban, prohibiting the manufacture and importation of nineteen types of semiautomatic assault weapons and high-capacity ammunition magazines. In the middle to late 1980s, the assault weapon became the weapon of choice for drug traffickers, street gangs, and paramilitary extremist groups. The ATF reports that although semiautomatic assault weapons constitute less than 1 percent of privately owned guns in America, they accounted for 8.4 percent of all firearms traced to crime in the years 1988 to 1991. Statistics indicate the use of assault weapons in crime has declined since the assault weapon ban went into effect.

Challenging Brady

In 1996, two rural sheriffs—handpicked by the NRA—challenged the constitutionality of the Brady Law before the U.S. Supreme Court. They based their challenge on the grounds that the Brady Law violated the Tenth Amendment, which distinguishes between state and federal powers. On June 27, 1997, the Supreme Court ruled that the federal government could not require state law enforcement to conduct Brady background checks but that state law enforcement could do them voluntarily. The Court let stand the other provisions of the Brady Law, including the five-day waiting period.

It is important to remember that the Court's decision was based solely on the Tenth Amendment and had nothing to do with the Second Amendment. The Supreme Court has long held that the Second Amendment concerns the protection of armed state-organized militias, not the personal ownership of guns for private use. Furthermore, the narrow effect of the decision had no impact on any of the other federal gun control laws.

The NRA, which had financed the court challenge to the Brady Act, declared victory. Its leaders claimed the Supreme Court decision had "fatally wounded" gun control laws by erecting an insurmountable constitutional barrier. Fortunately, this is hardly the case.

The waiting period is still in place, and more than 90 percent of law enforcement organizations across the country are continuing to conduct background checks of handgun purchasers. Recognizing that background checks are an important crime-fighting tool, the law enforcement community overwhelmingly supported the Brady bill and worked hard for its passage. That law enforcement organizations continue to perform background checks voluntarily is testament to the Brady Act's effectiveness.

Sensible Solutions

The gun lobby accuses Jim and me of trying to take guns away from law-abiding citizens. That is not true. Our goal is not to ban handguns or hunting weapons: our goal is to reduce firearm injuries and deaths through commonsense laws and regulations. We advocate laws that keep guns out of the hands of criminals, the mentally ill, and children.

We work for sensible regulations that protect public safety and prevent unintentional shootings. We believe that gun owners and gun manufacturers should take basic, commonsense precautions to safeguard the rest of society from the injuries, deaths, and costs caused by gun violence. Most people would be surprised to learn that there are more regulations governing the manufacture of a toy gun than the manufacture of a real gun! Common sense tells us that guns, like cars and washing machines, should be manufactured to conform to basic safety standards.

The NRA and its allies have tried to frighten and intimidate me; more important, they try to scare all Americans with tales, typically of an armed stranger confronting us in a dark alley, all in an effort to convince us we need to own a gun for protection. All we have to do is watch the news to see how many children are killed each year in unintentional shootings, how many deaths result from domestic violence, and how many people are killed with a gun in the heat of the moment by someone they know. Of course people should be concerned about the stranger in the dark alley. But the reality is that guns kept in the home are far more likely to be used to kill a family member or friend than to kill in self-defense.

Before I became involved with HCI, I thought I knew how Capitol Hill works because I had worked there. I was not prepared for the games, scare tactics, and massive spending from the gun lobby that kept the Brady bill from passing for seven years. When the Supreme Court struck down the background check provision of the Brady Act in 1997, I also learned that nothing is ever won forever—so I plan to keep on task.

A Safer Future

Legislation alone is not enough to put an end to gun injuries and deaths. Public attitudes and behavior surrounding guns have to change. I also chair HCI's sister organization, the Center to Prevent Handgun Violence (CPHV), which is devoted to preventing gun violence through public education. We have joined with parents and children, health professionals, educators, law enforcement officers, activists, clergy, members of the entertainment and legal professions, and many others to raise awareness about the dangers of guns in the home and in our communities. We teach children about the dangers of guns, work for gun industry reform through litigation, conduct research to track the effectiveness of gun laws, and work with the entertainment industry to deglamourize the use of guns in the media.

As a mother and former teacher, I believe that educating children about the dangers of guns is critical to creating a safer future for all Americans. CPHV has implemented the STAR program (Straight Talk About Risks) in over one thousand schools and youth programs nationwide to teach children alternatives to guns for solving problems. STAR has become the nation's premier gun violence prevention program for children in grades K–12.

We also created STOP (Steps to Prevent Firearm Injury) with the American Academy of Pediatrics. STOP enlists health professionals in counseling parents and children about the risks associated with guns in the home, just as they do about the dangers of household cleanser and prescription drugs.

All too often our children, our most precious resource, are the ones who fall victim to guns. In my travels around the country I have met too many parents who have lost a child to a carelessly stored gun in a neighbor's home. I have met too many children who are growing up afraid to play in their yards, walk to school, and sometimes even be in their own school because of the presence of guns. The fact is, the number of firearm deaths of children is twelve times higher in the United States than in twenty-five other industrialized nations combined. That reality is unacceptable, and I want it to change.

In 1968, Robert Kennedy shared his optimism about ending gun violence in America, not long after Martin Luther King Jr. was assassinated. Speaking to a crowd of supporters in Los Angeles, he said: "We are a great country, an unselfish country, and a compassionate country." Moments later an assassin's bullet took his life. After seeing yet another one of our nation's leaders fall victim to gunfire, Americans were fed up. The Gun Control Act of 1968—the most comprehensive set of gun control regulations at the time—was passed later that year.

Robert Kennedy's message is as valid now as it was in 1968: we are a compassionate and great country, and together we can end gun violence. Jim and I are full of hope because we believe that by working together, citizens can restore peace in our communities, eliminate gun violence, and preserve the American dream for the nation's families.

I think all of us have moments when we look at our lives and marvel that we have been led down paths we never thought we would take. For me, getting involved in the gun control movement did not feel like a choice. My personal experience compelled me to do it. My goal is to help make America's streets and homes safer for the next generation. Along the way, I have discovered the satisfaction that comes with trying to make a difference. The honor of working for a cause in which I truly believe has been its own reward.

BARBARA ROBERTS was governor of Oregon from 1991 to 1995, the first woman ever elected to that position. Most recently she has been director of the Program for Senior Executives in State and Local Government at the John F. Kennedy School of Government at Harvard University. A Democrat, she was elected Oregon's secretary of state in 1985, in which capacity she served until 1991. From 1981 to 1985, she was a member of the state house of representatives, where she served as majority leader in 1983 and 1984. Roberts is a former Multomah County commissioner and served ten years as an elected school board member and four years as an elected community college board member. A descendant of Oregon Trail pioneers, she attended Portland State University and Marylhurst College and holds an honorary doctorate from Willamette University.

Coloring
Outside the Lines

BARBARA ROBERTS

I HAVE A PLACE in history. Not only am I the first woman elected
governor in the state of Oregon but I am one of the first ten
women in American history to be elected governor in her own right.
Between 1974 and 1996, we ten cemented our place in history and
laid a foundation on which other women may build.

None of us will ever forget Ella Grasso of Connecticut, the first
woman elected governor in her own right, who served from 1974
until ill health forced her retirement in 1980. Next came Dixie Lee
Ray of Washington (1977–1981), Madeline Kunin of Vermont
(1985–1991), Martha Layne Collins of Kentucky (1984–1987), and
Kay Orr of Nebraska (1987–1991).

The election of 1990 was historic. Three women were elected governor: Ann Richards in Texas, Joan Finney in Kansas, and I in Oregon. All three of us held office from 1991 through 1995. Christine

Todd Whitman has been governor of New Jersey since 1994, and Jean Shaheen was elected governor of New Hampshire in 1996.

Six more women have been governors in our history, arriving by different routes; some were appointed and some succeeded their husbands. The first was Nellie Tayloe Ross of Wyoming (1925–1927), and the most recent is Jane Hull of Arizona, who was appointed in 1997.

Lest you believe that I and other women governors are some kind of a unique and special breed, let me assure you that we are not unlike millions of other women across this nation. As I have said hundreds of times, each of you is only one cause, one concern, one tragedy, one moral indignation away from active political involvement.

I began my political career as a citizen advocate, a parent seeking educational rights for my autistic son. My son had been sent home from school in the first grade—not for the day, but forever. His handicap meant he had no right to a public school education. I could not appeal—not to the school board, the courthouse, or the statehouse. The law gave my son no recognition, no rights, no recourse.

I simply could not accept the unfairness, the inequity, the fact that my son's disability would be exacerbated by his also being uneducated. I spoke out publicly about this injustice. I pleaded for help. I sought a hero. I waited for a leader to step forward to champion our children's cause.

A Mother's Cause

By the end of the 1960s, I was a divorced mother with two sons, no child support, and a low-paying office job. But I was unwilling to let these liabilities short-change my son any longer. I finally came to recognize that I had two crucial assets—a cause and a mother's anger! If I could not find the leader I sought, I would assume the position by self-appointment.

So I took one day a week off work (and the painful related pay cut), traveled to my state capitol, and began a fight for my son's educational rights. I was politically inexperienced, scared to death, and I didn't have the money to buy even a cup of coffee for a state legislator. But I marched up the capitol steps determined to change the world for the disabled children of my state.

Powerful education lobbyists worked against me every step of the way—the school boards association, the teachers organization, and the school administrators. They talked about the public cost, the disruption in classrooms and curriculum, the uselessness of learning time spent on children like my son. I fought back on the grounds of fairness and equity and the increased life-long potential for children with disabilities.

I carried my message to every state senator and every representative. I pleaded for my son's future. Finally, my son personally testified at a public legislative hearing. He told the senators that "special education" wasn't special for him. For him, it was all there was. The hearing concluded and the committee unanimously sent the legislation to the full senate for a vote. It passed the senate unanimously.

Five months later, Oregon had the first education rights law for emotionally handicapped children in the nation. A hearing at a time, a legislator at a time, letters from parents, grandparents, aunts and uncles, letters to newspapers, and countless hours in the marble halls of government—I had moved the mountain of government.

That first political success for my son cemented my belief that even if you are one person, if your cause is just and you are determined enough and if you can make your case well, you can make a difference in the political process. I learned it then; I believe it still.

That experience also taught me that silence is never golden on the issues of human rights, civil liberties, equity, fairness, and inclusion.

As a young, poor, divorced, politically unsophisticated woman, I had spoken out, and I had positively changed the lives of thousands of Oregon children and their families. My experience as a citizen advocate in my state legislature had also changed my life. I had a new success and a new direction. There was no turning back now that I knew what was possible.

A Citizen Advocate Moves Up

My new law gave educational rights to emotionally handicapped children and disbursed state funds to local school districts that initiated programs for these children. It provided for a statewide advisory committee and local committees to help plan and set policy for the new, special education programs. The law mandated the inclusion of school administrators, special education teachers, *and parents* of the disabled children.

I applied for, and was appointed to, the State Advisory Committee for Emotionally Handicapped Children, which was created by my new legislation. I was also placed on the Parkrose District Advisory Committee in my local school district. These two committees taught me a great deal about group policymaking and expanded my knowledge about state and local government. I had new confidence and new credentials.

My advisory committee experience helped tremendously when I first campaigned for public office. Within two years I was elected to my local school board, and a few years later ran successfully for my regional community college board. My work on those two boards gave me the community credentials and visibility to be chosen as a county commissioner to fill a one-year vacancy.

I had moved from citizen advocate to volunteer board member to elected office and, finally, to paid political office in the most populous county in Oregon. Each step of the way, my belief that one person can truly make a difference was reinforced.

My vote helped start the kindergarten program in my school district and the displaced worker program at the community college. Now as county commissioner, I voted to build the light rail line and strongly supported and voted for the comprehensive land use plan for the metropolitan region. I was making a difference.

The Outsider Moves Inside

During the early period of my political career, the women's movement was reaching full bloom for the second time in the twentieth century. Organizations like the National Women's Political Caucus, the National Organization for Women, the National Federation of Business and Professional Women's Clubs, the League of Women

Voters, and others were actively involved in advancing women's full participation in politics. They spoke up for women's rights, encouraged women to run for elective office, and changed the face of government in America. Many of their members worked on women's campaigns and sent money.

When the battle for the Equal Rights Amendment failed in 1982, the "war" continued. If we couldn't be included in the United States Constitution, we would be included on city councils, in state legislatures, in Congress, and in the governor's chair. I was one of those women! I was motivated, supported, and elected.

In 1980, I took my first step into state government by becoming a successful candidate for the state legislature. In one decade I had come from outsider to insider in the state capitol.

Now, when I walked up the capitol steps I was no longer a stranger to legislative members or to the legislative process. I knew I had a wonderful opportunity to make a difference on hundreds of issues. But if I believed the decade from 1970 to 1980 had dramatically changed my life, a crystal ball looking at 1990 would have taken my breath away!

In my second term in the Oregon House of Representatives, I became the first female house majority leader in the state's history. In 1984, I was elected statewide as secretary of state, becoming the first Democrat to hold the office in 110 years. In Oregon, the secretary of state is also the lieutenant governor and the state auditor. The office is considered a real political stepping stone. Four years later I was reelected, winning all thirty-six counties in the state. Not bad for an inexperienced citizen lobbyist!

In the spring of 1989, Oregon's governor withdrew as a candidate for reelection, a late and highly surprising political announcement. The following day I announced my candidacy in what political pundits and friends alike considered a futile race for governor.

But it wasn't the first time I had taken on an "impossible" effort against the odds in my state capital, or the first time I'd taken on part of the political power base. It wasn't the first time I'd watched the doubters smile, while some friends patted me on the head like a cute, imaginative child. It wasn't the first time I'd decided to change the world!

In November 1990, I did exactly that when I was elected the first woman governor in my state's history. On the day I was inaugurated, my family was there for the historic event—my mother, my sister, my two sons, my eighteen-month old granddaughter, and my state senator husband.

While waiting for the ceremonies to begin, my older son walked over, put his arm around my shoulder and said proudly, "Well, Mom, look at what I started!" My autistic son, now thirty-four years old with a high school diploma, a community college certificate, a job, and an apartment of his own, stood smiling at me, beaming at my great accomplishment.

Yet I knew more than anyone that it was he who deserved recognition for accomplishing the impossible. Or maybe, more accurately, it was what we had accomplished together that was worthy of note. He was my son, my cause, my inspiration. I was his mother, his protector, his advocate, and we each clearly had proven that one person does make a difference.

As I look back now on my twenty-five years in politics, I would describe it as a career committed to rattling the cage, challenging the status quo, pushing the envelope, and coloring outside the lines.

Over these challenging years, I have come to believe in risk-taking, in scar tissue, and in the road less traveled—and I am clearly not alone. Across this country, women are no longer willing to step aside to allow others to make decisions about their children, their communities, their states, their country, and their future. The huge changes for women in our culture inspire me, motivate me, and again turn me into a cheerleader for change.

I am so grateful to have lived in these times and to have been a participant in the political awakening of American women. I still believe that one person can make a difference, but I'm additionally convinced that women, together, can dramatically change the world.

TURNING POINTS

CHRISTINE TODD WHITMAN is governor of New Jersey. A Republican, she is the first woman governor of New Jersey and the first person to defeat an incumbent governor in a general election in modern state history. She was reelected for a second term in 1997. She appointed the first African American to the state supreme court, the first woman state supreme court chief justice, and the first woman state attorney general. She was honorary co-chair of the 1996 Republican National Convention. Whitman first ran for public office in 1982, when she was elected to the Somerset County Board of Freeholders, where she served until 1987. She was president of the New Jersey Board of Public Utilities from 1988 to 1990. Whitman holds a B.A. degree from Wheaton College in Massachusetts.

My Moral Compass

CHRISTINE TODD WHITMAN

E VERY ONE OF US has a moral compass. It may go by other names—conscience, inner voice, sense of right and wrong—but it's there.

I like the term *moral compass* because it reminds me of the tool navigators and explorers have long used to find their way. Life is certainly a journey that requires the skill of a navigator and the bold courage of an explorer. Without a moral compass to guide our way, we risk becoming hopelessly lost.

Each of us uses our own moral compass every day to make decisions—sometimes large, mostly small. Perhaps it helps in deciding whether to purchase an under-twelve movie ticket for your thirteen-year-old child. Maybe it guides you as you glide up to a stop sign at an empty intersection. Or perhaps it points you in the right direction when you are tempted to blame a software glitch for the paper or report you don't have ready in time.

When confronted with the small issues, it's all too easy to ignore the direction one's moral compass is pointing. Rationalizations come so readily when the matter at hand is small and apparently inconsequential. But to those who strive to follow their moral compasses, even the small deviations can weigh heavily.

I have asked some friends whether they can recall specific instances of ignoring their own moral compasses. I have been amazed at how quickly they can recall—and that so many of their recollections have been about seemingly little things that happened many years ago.

Everyone agrees, however, that the lesson they carried away from those experiences is that you have to be consistent in doing the little things right to have any hope of doing the big things right. My own experience confirms the wisdom of that observation.

Perhaps the biggest challenge my moral compass ever faced occurred literally hours after I was elected governor in 1993. Let me set the scene.

In 1990, I lost a very close race for United States Senate to Bill Bradley—a star in the Democratic Party and a candidate every pundit, analyst, and observer believed would crush me on election day. To everyone's surprise, Senator Bradley found I was a tough nut to crack, and although I didn't win, I was immediately positioned as the Republican front-runner for governor in 1993 against incumbent governor Jim Florio.

After much careful analysis and deliberation, I decided to make that run. Once I reached that decision, I went full-tilt toward my goal. Nearly every waking hour—and more than a few sleepless nights—were dedicated to the race.

Campaigning is hard work and it takes a toll, physically, mentally, and emotionally. But spending time one-on-one with people going about their everyday lives reaffirms my sense that government has an important, if limited, role in helping families, businesses, and communities succeed. It's also reaffirming to hear from people for whom our efforts are paying off—like the woman who approached me at a 1997 campaign event, hugged me, and said, "I'm in Work First [our welfare reform program] and I'm on my way to a job!"

By the time election day 1993 rolled around, I was exhausted. We finished the campaign with a ten-day bus tour that crisscrossed New Jersey from early morning to late evening. Finally, I reached the finish line—and crossed it first, becoming the first challenger to defeat an incumbent governor in the general election in modern New Jersey history.

The taste of victory was sweet. I enjoyed it—and I was hoping to enjoy it for more than just a day. That, however, was not to be.

An Outrageous Lie

Two days after the election, our campaign's most prominent strategist went to a breakfast meeting with a roomful of reporters. For reasons that I will never understand, he told those reporters that the key to my victory was his brilliant effort to suppress the voter turnout among urban blacks by, in effect, bribing African American religious leaders in those communities.

Until I draw my last breath, I will remember how the news of this outrageous lie knocked the wind out of me. I knew—for a certainty— that my campaign would not have done this and did not do this. It was simply inconceivable. I quickly confirmed my belief by talking to those involved in my campaign—including our so-called strategic genius. Everyone assured me that my campaign had done no such thing.

Our strong denials, however, did nothing to extinguish the firestorm that erupted. Understandably, the media, our opponents, and the state's black clergy members wanted a full investigation. Not only did this story impugn the integrity of my campaign, it also smeared the reputations of those religious leaders who stood accused of accepting bribes for keeping down the vote in their communities.

I knew I had to act quickly—not so much to secure my victory but to restore my integrity. Some suggested that I brand the calls for an investigation as nothing more than a partisan effort to reverse the election. Others maintained that I should move forward with putting my administration together, ignoring the serious questions that had been raised. My own moral compass, however, was pointing in another direction.

I decided that there was only one honorable course to take. I announced that I would delay my inauguration so long as there was any credible evidence that my campaign had subverted the electoral process. I could not—and would not—assume office under the cloud that my campaign had somehow stolen the election.

I always believed that it wasn't healthy to spend too much time reveling in the thrill of victory. But take my word for it, there must be better ways to come back down to earth. It wasn't easy to offer up my victory voluntarily as the price to pay if these charges proved to be true—but it was the right thing to do.

The weeks that followed were filled with the most extensive electoral investigation ever conducted in the state of New Jersey. Not a single piece of evidence was ever found to support the charge that we had bribed our way to victory. That is because we hadn't.

Conscience and Controversy

Of course, had things developed differently, I would probably not be governor today—and I would not deserve to be. The decision not to assume office would not have been forced upon me—I would have made it voluntarily. Although I might not have been able to live in the governor's mansion, I would have been able to live with myself.

The news media have a way of holding onto controversial stories, so virtually every article since then that has been written about any of my dealings with African American leaders has included a few paragraphs about the fabricated payoff.

Not surprisingly, the controversy continues to affect my relationship with the African American community. In my successful bid for reelection in 1997, I received a significantly smaller percentage of the African American vote than I received in 1993. I was encouraged, however, by endorsements from several prominent members of the state's African American clergy.

The aftermath of the 1993 election was one case in which the truth of Harper Lee's observation in *To Kill a Mockingbird* was literally true. She wrote: "The one thing that doesn't abide by majority rule is a person's conscience." The hundreds of thousands of votes I had received would not have been enough to defeat the single vote my conscience had cast.

I am convinced that the reason I was able to follow my moral compass at this turning point in my life was because I had lots of practice. I was ready to do what was right when it really counted because I always tried to do what was right when it barely counted. Clearly, the credit for that belongs not so much to me as it does to those whose model I have tried to follow, including my parents, friends, and teachers.

In fact, keeping my word to the African American community in the aftermath of the 1993 scandal was, in a small way, a matter of keeping a family tradition. My parents and grandparents had always taught me that you are only as good as your word. They pointed to the example of an ancestor named Isaac Reeve, who graduated from West Point in 1835 and served on the Union side in the Civil War. Lieutenant Colonel Reeve was captured in Texas during the war by his best friend from West Point, who was fighting for the Confederacy.

During Lt. Col. Reeve's imprisonment, his daughter died, and his friend gave him compassionate leave to return to New York. But he had to make a difficult promise to his friend: he would not go back into combat for the Union for the remainder of the war, no matter how committed he was to the Union.

Once Lt. Col. Reeve was back in New York, the Union tried hard to reenlist him, but he appealed all the way up to the White House for relief from duty. He believed strongly in the Union cause, but he had made a promise in good faith and viewed it as a matter of conscience that he honor that promise.

General Winfield Scott sent a memo to President Lincoln recommending that Lt. Col. Reeve not break the conditions of his parole. President Lincoln, my family taught me, believed that the best way an American could serve his country was to keep his word. On the bottom of General Scott's memo, Lincoln wrote, "I approve the above opinion."

I would like to think President Lincoln would have approved of the way I handled this turning point in my own life.

PATSY T. MINK is the member of Congress for the Second District of Hawaii. A Democrat, she was first elected to the House in 1965, serving until 1977, and was elected again in 1990. From 1977 to 1978, she was an assistant secretary of state and from 1978 to 1981, she served as the national president of Americans for Democratic Action. From 1956 through 1959, she held elected positions as a representative and then a senator in the territorial legislature of Hawaii, which became the fiftieth state in 1959. From 1962 to 1964, Mink was a member of the Hawaii State Senate. She served on the Honolulu City Council from 1983 to 1987, which she chaired from 1983 to 1985. She holds a B.A. degree from the University of Hawaii, a J.D. degree from the University of Chicago Law School, and numerous honorary degrees.

A Change in Plans

PATSY T. MINK

I WAS BORN in the small sugar plantation town of Paia, on the island of Maui, in the year 1927. Maui is one of seven inhabited islands of Hawaii. Hawaii was annexed to the United States of
America in 1898 and became an incorporated territory. My father,
Suematsu, and my mother, Mitama, were both born in Hawaii and
were natural-born citizens of the United States of America.

My dad was one of the earliest graduates of the University of
Hawaii. He was born on the island of Kauai and was orphaned at
a very young age. His older brother worked in a pineapple cannery
to help pay for my father's education. My dad moved to Honolulu
to attend a private Christian boarding school, known then as Mills
School, and then went on to the University of Hawaii. In 1922,
he graduated from the University of Hawaii with a degree in civil
engineering.

My father accepted a job as a land surveyor on the island of Maui for the East Maui Irrigation Company, which was a subsidiary of the Maui Agricultural Company. His first task was to help design and construct an irrigation ditch bringing water from East Maui to the rich cane fields in central Maui. While working in the deep country of east Maui, he met my mother and they were married soon thereafter on July 23, 1924. They had two children, my older brother, Eugene, and me.

My mother was born on Maui in 1905, one of eleven children. She, along with her five sisters, graduated from Maunaolu Seminary, which was also a Christian boarding school administered by the Congregational Church. Her five brothers all were able to attend schools on Maui. Despite growing up in the remote reaches of Maui, her parents knew the value of education and through the generosity of well-to-do neighbors provided all their children with a basic education.

As a college graduate, my father was considered part of management, although he was not really paid as such. But we were given a grand company house to live in and enjoyed many privileges not ordinarily given to the other plantation workers. However, we always knew our place. After all, we were not white, as all the bosses were.

The widowed manager of the company had a young daughter with whom I was allowed to play because we lived across the street from one another. When her father remarried, those visits were halted, and I saw little of my friend after that.

We lived a very rural life, enjoying the outdoors and the simple elements of family life. I knew very little about the greater world. All I knew was that I wanted to be like my father and attend college. Ever since I could recall, I wanted to become a medical doctor. I looked up to our plantation doctor who took care of me, and decided that was what I wanted to be most of all.

I finished high school in 1944. With the onset of World War II and the bombing of Pearl Harbor, those were years of great turmoil and uncertainty. I was sixteen years old when I entered the University of Hawaii as a freshman. I majored in zoology and was determined to complete premedical studies so that I could enter medical school. I joined the premedical clubs and steadfastly pursued my goal to become a doctor.

No one had ever told me that women were not being admitted to medical school. The thought that I would be excluded on account of my sex never crossed my mind. I thought that maybe I couldn't score high enough or maybe I couldn't raise enough money to pay the tuition, but it never occurred to me that there were insurmountable barriers that would prevent me from reaching my goal.

A Change of Plans

As my senior year approached, I began applying for medical schools. I must have sent away applications to at least a dozen of them. Every one came back with a rejection. Most said that they did not accept female students. I was absolutely dumbfounded.

After four years of college, I had a B.A. degree that could not get me into medical school! It could not even get me a job in the sciences. Upon graduation from the University of Hawaii I went to work as a clerk typist at Hickman Air Force Base. That job lasted a few weeks.

I quit and applied for a job as an assistant to the director in the Honolulu Academy of Arts. I was astounded when I was hired. There I met a wonderful woman, Mrs. Arthur Restarick, who took me in and helped me see that my world had not ended with my exclusion from medical school. She suggested that I try other graduate schools.

What? I had studied exclusively in one field and with one goal in mind. What could I possibly do? She suggested law school. I was game and decided that I couldn't lose anything by trying. So I wrote away to two law schools: Columbia University School of Law and the University of Chicago Law School.

This was already the middle of summer in the year 1948. Columbia University School of Law replied saying they were sorry but the class entering in the fall was already filled; that was understandably so. The University of Chicago Law School, however, replied that I was accepted and that I could enroll in their fall 1948 class.

I knew that my father could not afford to send me to this prestigious school and that I had to have a full tuition scholarship at the very minimum. My dad, at age fifty, had left the plantation and moved to Honolulu to start his own business. Money was very tight. My mother, who had never worked outside the home before, found it necessary to work to help with the expenses.

Looking over the University of Chicago Law School's financial aid information, I came across a scholarship that was available to students whose fathers were veterans of World War I. My dad was an honorably discharged veteran of World War I. I applied, and received a full tuition scholarship for the three years I attended the University of Chicago Law School.

This was the turning point in my life. I literally turned from defeat and disillusionment that I could not become a doctor, to an entirely new adventure—that of becoming a lawyer.

I graduated from the University of Chicago Law School in 1951 with a doctor of law degree. I returned home to Hawaii in the summer of 1952, married and with a baby daughter, Gwendolyn.

From then on began the story of the rest of my life as a lawyer-politician–public servant.

A Front Row Seat

With my law degree I had expected ready access to employment. That was not the case, however. In fact, everywhere I went for a job I was turned away because I was a woman, because I was a married woman, and because I had a baby. In almost every case I was told explicitly that those were the reasons I was not being hired. To do so today would be illegal, but back then it was commonplace to exclude women from professional employment on the grounds of their sex alone, without any other justification whatsoever.

Additionally, I was not even permitted to take the bar examination because, I was told, by marrying on the mainland I had lost my legal residence in Hawaii. I was informed that I had to wait three years before I could apply. The attorney general's office stated that I had acquired my husband's domicile of Pennsylvania when I married him in Chicago. I submitted legal memoranda refuting this exclusionary rule and finally won their agreement that under the law I never lost my Hawaii residency, since I never assumed my husband's state of domicile.

Without an employment opportunity I decided to open up my own law office at 12 North King Street in Honolulu. It was extremely difficult. Clients were few and far between, and those who came had little money to spare. To help with the expenses of private practice, I obtained a teaching position at the University of Hawaii, College of Business Administration.

Meanwhile Hawaii was undergoing a great political upheaval. Veterans of World War II were returning home as much decorated heroes. They were engaged in changing the politics of special privileges to a more egalitarian and open forum. Never overwhelmed by any large number of clients, I was able to join in this crusade for change.

I attended numerous meetings where our platform was developed. I organized young people to become involved in political change. As a lawyer I had inherent authority to participate. I could speak with genuine knowledge. I did not have to fight my way to the table. I had a front row seat with the title doctor of law. When I spoke, people listened. The more I learned about politics, the greater my confidence that I could become an active participant.

There is no doubt that for me the turning point in my life was having the opportunity to attend law school and to become an attorney. It opened all the doors that previously had been shut. With my law degree, all I needed was the will, the stamina, the courage, and the determination to become a public servant. The rest is history.

TIPPER GORE is the second lady of the United States. She is mental health policy adviser to the president, special adviser to the Interagency Council on the Homeless, and a co-founder of Families for the Homeless, a nonpartisan organization that raises public awareness of homeless issues. She forged a partnership with the National Mental Health Association to produce the major photographic exhibit "Homeless in America," which toured the nation. She formerly worked as a newspaper photographer for the *Nashville Tennessean*. A strong proponent of exercise, she jogs, bikes, hikes, skis, and rollerblades. She holds a B.A. degree from Boston University and an M.S. degree from George Peabody College at Vanderbilt University.

The Power of Partnership

TIPPER GORE

P EOPLE NEVER QUITE KNOW how to introduce me. Sometimes they call me the second lady. Sometimes they refer to me as the second first lady. Once I was even introduced as the second lady of vice. Maybe no one has ever given the wife of the vice president of the United States a title because the position is so poorly defined. There's no job description, no pay, no career path, and limited opportunities for promotion. The way I see it, this post is an opportunity to further the causes I believe in.

In that respect, my life now is not so different from what it used to be. For years I have been advocating better treatment for those

From *Picture This*, by Tipper Gore. Copyright © 1996 by Tipper Gore. Used by permission of Broadway Books, a division of Bantam Doubleday Dell Publishing Group.

with mental illness, for people who are homeless, and for children generally. The main difference is that as the wife of the vice president, my voice on behalf of these communities has a broader reach. My priorities are the same too: my husband, Al, and our four terrific children come first. In other ways, though, my life has changed radically since Bill Clinton and my husband won the 1992 election.

Inevitably I am a lot of different things to different people. I am a mother of four children. I am a wife. I am a daughter and a daughter-in-law. Also I have my official role in the administration and my volunteer roles. But one thing that I have engaged in and loved that is completely separate from any of those other pursuits and people is photography.

The Making of a Photographer

When our first child, Karenna, was born in 1973, Al was working as a journalist on the night shift at the Nashville *Tennessean*. During the day, he was attending first Vanderbilt Divinity School and then law school. Meanwhile, I was feeling the need to do something for myself in addition to staying at home with our baby.

Al had given me my first real camera—a 35 mm Yashica—and he and Nancy Rhoda, a good friend and professional photographer, both encouraged me to take a course in photography. I commuted one hundred miles to take a class with Jack Corn, the photo editor at the *Tennessean,* and learned everything from the principles of photojournalism to printing and processing pictures.

Evidently Jack saw something in my work, because he offered me a part-time job at the *Tennessean*. I started out in a photo lab, developing film, and progressed to printing pictures and, finally, shooting them. After a while, I began doing photo essays, taking the pictures and writing the text. When the paper published them, it was a huge thrill. For instance, the paper ran my picture of an evicted woman sitting in the rain; afterward, scores of people called in offering to help, reinforcing my understanding of the power of photography to inspire and motivate.

While working at the *Tennessean,* I was also going to graduate school, studying for my master's degree in psychology. I was planning to become a therapist, even though I felt more and more drawn to photography. And then Al dropped his bombshell. One Friday in March 1976, he told me that he was thinking of running for Congress.

At this time, I thought Al was going to become either a writer or a lawyer. But that very morning we learned that the seat of the Fourth Congressional District in Tennessee—the district where he grew up and we owned the farm—was being vacated. Three days later he announced his candidacy, and our lives changed forever.

Al was raised in a political family. His father had served in Congress for many years, and Al had always been fascinated by politics. It was clearly too good a chance to pass up. Though I understood his decision, my feelings were mixed. I had just attended a seminar on photography in Atlanta, and I was eager to keep on learning.

I was as happy as I had ever been—I loved taking pictures for the *Tennessean*—and at first I said I would only campaign for Al on my days off. But Jack Corn talked some sense into me. "Tipper," he said, "this is the chance of a lifetime. I think Al can actually win, but you really need to get out there and work with him. And don't worry. If he does lose, your job will still be here."

Part of my reluctance, I suppose, came from not wanting to be totally swept up in Al's life just at that moment when a professional career of my own was beckoning. But Al and I had operated as a team since the early days of our marriage, and there was no way I could feel comfortable doing anything but whole-heartedly supporting him at this important moment in his life. We had meant too much to each other for too long.

My Family

Unfortunately, I was not what you would call a natural politician. Even though Al's father, Albert Gore Sr., had been in the Senate for many years, and even though I had helped in his last campaign some years earlier, it was agony for me to go up to strangers and ask them to vote for my husband. I could be embarrassed very easily and had to work to become comfortable in my role as a political spouse.

Family has always been supremely important to me. Al and I both came from very small families, and early on we agreed that we wanted six children when we got married. I was an only child, and my parents were divorced when I was four.

After the divorce, my mother and I went to live with my grandmother and my grandfather, who was a banker. I adored them, and they adored me. They were the first to call me Tipper—my given name is Mary Elizabeth—a nickname that comes from a lullaby my mother used to sing to me. I certainly didn't lack for attention with all those adults doting on me. I also remained close to my father and his family, who lived nearby. But I envied my friends who had brothers and sisters to live with.

Without question, the biggest event of my youth was meeting Al. I was sixteen, he was seventeen. We were introduced to each other at his high school graduation dance, and he called the next day to invite me to a party that weekend. I'll never forget it: we put on a record and danced and danced. It was just like everyone else melted away. And that was it. We've been together ever since.

We both went to college in the Boston area. He went to Harvard, where he studied government. Not long ago, I was going through some old letters from him when he was a freshman at Harvard and I was still in high school and planning to visit him in Cambridge. The problem was that my grandmother planned to come along as a chaperone. "Does she really have to come?" he asked. "I just want to be with you." But my grandmother came all the same, and Al behaved like a perfect gentleman.

I got a degree in psychology from Boston University, and that spring, after I graduated from college, we got married. That was almost thirty years ago, and I can honestly say that Al and I are still in love—now more than ever.

We share many interests, such as our concern for the environment and our desire for a deeper spirituality in our daily lives. We both like physical activity and being out-of-doors; whenever possible we run together. We're avid moviegoers, and we love jazz and rock 'n' roll, but neither of us is a big party-goer.

Our Partnership

I believe the secret to success of our marriage is the way we view each other as partners. Al has supported me in everything I've undertaken. I've done the same for him. When he was in Congress, for example, I could have begun pursuing my own ambitions again.

I have lots of friends whose husbands are in the Senate and the House who have their own full-time careers. Although they may go to an occasional luncheon for congressional spouses or a White House Christmas party, that's about as involved as they get in their husbands' political careers, and I respect their choices.

But right from the beginning, Al wanted me to go on that journey in his life, so I plunged right in. It was a great opportunity to put some of my social concerns into action. Working with congressional friends, for example, I formed a task force to study violence on television and its effects on children. We issued a report and delivered it to Congress.

If anything, the experience of Al's being vice president has made us even closer. We have shared so much, so intensely, since 1992—the campaigns, the inaugurations, the great responsibilities the president has placed on Al's shoulders—that it's deepened the intimacy between us. There is more of a sense of unity to our work life too. Some of the ceremonial duties that come with Al's job are duties best performed by a couple—a husband and wife, each with a role to play.

My Crusades

I am something of a crusader at heart, and I worked hard at the causes I espoused. In Tennessee, I started a program called Tennessee Voices for Children, bringing together professionals in the field of mental health to press for more progressive policies. To cite just one example of our achievements, we advocated for a program called Home Ties, which delivers services in the home rather that in an institutional setting. Before that, Tennessee had a disproportionately high number of children with mental illness in state custody. Today, that number has been cut by two-thirds.

I've also spent a lot of time working on the issue of homelessness, an interest for which I can credit my children. One day in the early eighties, when Al was still in Congress, I was driving the kids home after having lunch with him at the Capitol. We stopped for a traffic light about one block away and saw a homeless woman standing on the curb, talking to herself and gesturing.

Homelessness on a large scale was still fairly rare at the time, and the kids were shocked. "Mom, what's wrong with her?" they asked. "Why is she talking to herself?" I told them that she was probably mentally ill and she might be hearing voices. "We can't leave her here," they said. "Let's take her home with us. This is terrible." I had to tell them we would do something.

That evening at dinner, we talked about it with Al, and all of us became determined to help. The children began volunteering by making sandwiches for kids at Martha's Table, a local provider for homeless families. Al held hearings in Tennessee about homelessness and held a statewide conference on the problem.

I put my photographer's mind to work and organized a traveling photographic exhibit called "Homeless in America," which put a human face on the numbing statistics. I wanted those pictures to move people into action in their own communities. Later, I began volunteering with an organization called Health Care for the Homeless, going out with their van to provide medical care to mentally ill people living on the streets.

I am a great believer in helping those in need one-on-one. You're much more effective that way, and the satisfaction you get is much greater when you personally give of yourself. If you never do more than write a check, if you never connect directly with the people you want to help, you will do some good, but you will never feel as fulfilled as you will if you take the time to forge a real relationship.

There were times when my crusades landed me in hot water. The one that created the most controversy was the campaign to get the record industry to warn parents about violent and obscene lyrics. It all started one day in 1985, when I listened to a song my eleven-year-old daughter had just bought and was shocked to discover how explicit the lyrics were.

Not long afterward, Susan Baker (whose husband was then Ronald Reagan's treasury secretary) and I joined forces to form the Parents Music Resource Center (PMRC). We decided to start a consumer movement to put pressure on the record industry to adopt a warning label for violence, profanity, and sexually explicit lyrics.

Luckily, Al has never expected me to be a politically safe wife. When he first got elected, we made a pledge. We said, "Let's never do anything we really don't believe in, even if it means losing an election." And though some people might find this hard to believe, he never once asked me to distance myself from the PMRC campaign. On the contrary, he always said, "Keep it up. You're doing the right thing. I don't care what people say."

Ultimately, our efforts produced a victory. The recording industry eventually did adopt a voluntary warning label, and I think we were able to alert parents that behind their backs commercial interests were bombarding children and teenagers with sexually explicit and violent entertainment. I know for sure that we started a national conversation on college campuses and at dinner tables across the country. And a lot of people changed their minds. Even today, people come up to me and say, "I really like what you did. It was very, very important to me."

Behind the Scenes

Having spent sixteen years in public life before the 1992 election, I thought I'd be able to make a fairly smooth transition to life as the vice president's wife. The children were also pretty accustomed to the demands of public life.

But nothing really prepares you for the loss of privacy that goes with a position like this. It's not just the presence of household staff or the Secret Service agents. It's the intense interest of the news media. Once, our family went bowling, and the *New York Times* printed each of our scores the next morning. We haven't been able to get the kids to go bowling with us since then.

This kind of scrutiny is hard enough on adults, but it's particularly unfair to children. They don't know the background. All they know is the limelight can be very harsh, and they don't like it. So I have fought hard to give our children some privacy and to make life here at the "official residence" feel as normal as possible.

I'm often asked how I spend my time these days, and the first thing I say is I'm lucky because no two days are alike. One day, I might make appearances in three different states. Another I might be scheduled to visit schools, homeless shelters, or work sites for mentally ill people. Often, I am called on to perform official duties, like accompanying Al on trips abroad. We do a fair amount of official entertaining, and the Clintons have always graciously included us in state functions.

As a card-carrying member of this administration, I also try to do my part for the Democratic ticket. I gave a lot of speeches at the request of the Democratic National Committee, and I chair the Women's Leadership Forum (WLF), a Democratic group that encourages women to take part in the political process. That translates to many meetings and receptions and traveling to states on behalf of the WLF.

A Labor of Love

Many of my speeches are related to my role as the adviser to the president on mental health. This position came about as a result of all the time I spent with the Clintons on a bus during the 1992 presidential campaign, when the president discovered how passionate I am on the subject of mental health.

One of the points I try to get across when I speak about mental illness is that treatment actually works. If someone has a broken bone, no one ever questions that with proper treatment it will eventually heal. But people have not yet realized how much progress has been made in managing and curing mental illness.

The data show high levels of success in treating everything from substance abuse to chronic depression to schizophrenia. For one thing, new pharmaceutical breakthroughs have made a big difference. When doctors use a combination of medication and therapy, the cure rate for schizophrenia is now over 60 percent. For depression it's 80 percent! If statistics such as these were widely known, the insurance industry would no longer have any excuse for refusing to pay psychiatric bills for people who are suicidal or so depressed they can't work or take care of their children.

My interest in the field of mental health goes back to my own childhood, when my mother suffered from serious bouts of depression. This was bad enough, but the situation was made worse by her fears that someone would find out, because at that time the stigma associated with mental illness was so enormous.

Once, when my mother was in the hospital for something else, I wanted to tell the doctors about the medication she was taking. But she was so terribly fearful of someone finding out—even a doctor—that she wouldn't let me tell them. It broke my heart. For decades, she suffered in silence; only in recent years has she been able to speak openly about her experience.

As the president's adviser on mental health issues, I am working hard to destigmatize mental illness. One of the things I'm proudest of is having prodded the government to change the way it handles the subject of mental illness in the hiring process.

Among other things, applicants no longer have to disclose whether they've had family or marriage counseling. Furthermore, the question, "Have you ever seen a psychiatrist?" is no longer placed next to the one asking, "Have you ever committed a felony?" In addition, information not relevant to the hiring process must remain confidential.

The brain, after all, is a part of the body. Why should we discriminate against a disorder that emanates from the brain? Why should mental illness be put in a completely different category from a disease of the lung, the liver, or the heart?

Not long ago, someone asked me what I wanted to be remembered for. I said I wanted to be remembered as a wife, a mother, and an advocate for mental health and the homeless. I also want to be remembered as someone who enjoyed life. This may sound frivolous, but just about everybody needs to take more time to have fun. People work too hard, and they take themselves too seriously. They should go rollerblading once in a while, like I do. As the kids say: Get a life!

Washington is particularly rough on people in politics, which in recent years has become increasingly vicious. For too many people, the rules of engagement today are simple but brutal: take no prisoners. The combatants want to win at any cost, so they wind up calling each other names instead of arguing the issues on their merits.

I want to help bring back civility and a sense of fun, and I deliberately try to lighten the atmosphere around me. I think it is extremely important to remember that there is so much joy in life. Al and I have often said that we need to work hard, but we need to celebrate each other too. I cherish every moment with him and my children, and I thank God for the opportunity I've been given to make a difference on behalf of people's lives.

POLLY B. BACA is the chief executive officer of Sierra Baca Systems, a management consulting firm. A member of the Colorado legislature for twelve years, she was first elected to the state house in 1974 and the state senate in 1978. She was the first minority woman elected to the state senate and the first Hispanic woman to serve in the leadership of any state senate in the nation. One of the original inductees of the National Hispanic Hall of Fame, she was regional administrator of the General Services Administration, Rocky Mountain Region VIII, from 1994 to 1998. Baca formerly was director of the U.S. Office of Consumer Affairs, executive director of the Colorado Hispanic Institute, and vice chair of the Democratic National Committee. She holds a B.A. degree from Colorado State University and honorary degrees from the University of Northern Colorado at Greeley and Wartburg College.

Seasons of a Life

POLLY B. BACA

WHEN I WAS THREE years old I had an experience that shaped the rest of my life. On a beautiful spring Sunday morning as our family arrived at church in Greeley, Colorado, I noticed little girls in pretty white dresses preparing to parade around the church. I wanted to watch them, but even standing on a kneeler I could barely see over the pew. So I persuaded my parents to sit in the center aisle instead of the side aisle, so I could better see the little girls.

Before long a church usher came over and told us we were not allowed to sit in the center aisle. The church was segregated. Mexicans and Mexican Americans were not permitted to sit in the center aisle, only in the side aisles. At that moment I realized my family was different; to me it meant we were "not as good as" other people.

The pain of that experience has been the driving force of my life. At first, I was determined to change the way people treat Mexican

Americans by proving we are bright and capable; that matured into a commitment to help improve the way all people treat each other.

As a victim of ethnic discrimination, I learned how important it is not to prejudge others. That was the first of many valuable lessons that have served me well throughout my life.

Networking Pays Off

As early as grade school, I believed I had a God-given mission to prove that Mexican Americans were as bright and capable as anyone else. By the time I was in high school I settled down and worked for good grades to win a college scholarship in pursuit of this mission. My parents couldn't afford a college education for three daughters. Besides, it was not the thing to do. Friends criticized my parents for even talking about sending their daughters to college. "Why waste all that money?" they asked. "After all they're just going to go off and get married." Fortunately, my parents didn't heed the criticism.

I enrolled at Colorado State University in Fort Collins, thirty miles from Greeley, which seemed like a long distance from home at the time. At nineteen I won an internship with the state Democratic party during the 1960 presidential campaign. I was awed by young senator John F. Kennedy and his two brothers, Robert and Edward. I worked around the clock during the campaign, which gave me an opportunity to meet many Kennedy operatives who came through Colorado.

One was Carlos McCormick, who had organized the first "Viva Kennedy" campaign. After I graduated from college, Carlos arranged an interview for me with the director of research and education for an international labor union. The director offered me a job in Washington, D.C., as an editorial assistant for the union newspaper. I wanted to say no but couldn't. I knew that such an opportunity did not come along often—especially for young Mexican

American women—and I felt strongly that I had a responsibility to other women and minorities to accept the job. In December 1962, I left home to work for the International Brotherhood of Pulp, Sulphite, and Paper Mill Workers.

I learned two new lessons: one, networking pays off; two, be a risk-taker. Taking a risk can lead to some incredibly exciting life adventures.

Be a Risk-Taker

Both good and bad experiences beset my early career, ranging from being sexually harassed to learning valuable skills, being a part of historic events, and interacting with some of the most interesting people in the world. My three years with the Pulp, Sulphite, and Paper Mill Workers and then two years with the Brotherhood of Railway and Airline Clerks taught me the art of lobbying and the real world of politics in the nation's capital.

But I yearned to help Mexican Americans still suffering the blows of bigotry in the Southwest. In the fall of 1965, I met Cesar Chavez and began spending my free time with the D.C. *Huelga* (Strike) Committee in support of the farm workers' movement. The following year, I met Luis Valdez and the *Teatro Campesino* cast and helped sponsor fund-raisers for the "cause." Soon I began to question my "safe" role with the labor movement and longed to become more directly involved in the Civil Rights movement.

When the 1966 Civil Rights Leadership Conference was held at the White House, Mexican Americans were not invited. President Lyndon Johnson tried to correct the oversight by hosting several meetings with Mexican American leaders in the Southwest. As a result, the White House InterAgency Committee on Mexican Americans was created. My networking and risk-taking lessons came into play, and I was offered a position as the new agency's public information officer.

This was an opportunity to get directly involved with the movement to help Mexican Americans. My friends cautioned me not to become a "professional Mexican." I ignored their advice and eagerly accepted the job.

Live Each Day to the Fullest

The White House position wasn't close enough to the "people" for me. The 1968 presidential campaign was under way, and when Robert F. Kennedy announced his candidacy, I joined the campaign staff. Because of Kennedy's commitment to civil rights, I spent my spare time with Mexican American leaders working on Martin Luther King Jr.'s 1968 Poor Peoples' March.

When news came on April 4, 1968, of King's assassination and rioting broke out in Washington, I ventured into the riot area with a friend to volunteer at a church. We narrowly escaped being dragged into a car by intoxicated teenagers, thanks to a cab driver who rescued us. Never have I gotten such a tongue-lashing from a good Samaritan. The cab driver's warning taught me a new lesson: in taking risks to help others, be careful not to endanger your life or the lives of those around you.

Soon I was assigned to Los Angeles as deputy director of the "Viva Kennedy" campaign. It was an exciting campaign but with a tragic ending at the Ambassador Hotel. Senator Kennedy's assassination on June 5, 1968, left an indelible mark on my psyche. For the first time, I truly recognized that the only certainty is change; life is fragile, and it is important to live each day to the fullest.

Disillusioned and despondent over the death of my hero, I helped the farm workers organize their memorial mass and left Los Angeles for the funeral at St. Patrick's Cathedral in New York City. That long, somber day ended at Arlington cemetery where, as a member of the staff, I was able to say my personal good-byes to Senator Kennedy. After helping close the campaign offices, I decided to leave politics and return to Denver.

On the way home I took a detour to Venezuela and Central America. Had I consulted anyone, I would have been told that it wasn't safe for a young woman to travel by herself in foreign countries. To my delight, caring families and individuals came to my rescue. I had precious encounters with loving souls who took pity on my broken Spanish and helped me. I discovered the universal beauty of the human spirit, regardless of national boundaries or local political turmoil.

After returning to Colorado, I made plans to join friends at the 1968 Democratic National Convention in Chicago. The convention began as an opportunity to practice my lesson that networking pays off. But the events that transpired convinced me it was time to follow my heart and try to make a difference in the lives of those I had left behind. On the night of the major confrontation between anti-Vietnam demonstrators and the Chicago police, I participated in a peace march to the hotel that served as convention headquarters. Fortunately, I decided to go inside the hotel across the street to look at the television coverage of the convention.

A great commotion began on the street. We rushed to the windows and saw the police in military formation charge the crowd below, with night sticks swinging. Horrified, I realized I had just missed the encounter. My angels must have be watching over me. I knew then my life would never be the same. I knew I had to work to change the way people treat each other.

My Cause, My Love

After Robert Kennedy's death, I had talked to Cesar Chavez about working with the farm workers for $5 a week. At the convention I talked to Dolores Huerta, who worked with Chavez, and told her I was ready to fulfill that pledge and move to Delano, California.

As I prepared to go, I received a phone call from Henry Santiestevan, who had been my supervisor in the Kennedy campaign. He was thrilled that the Ford Foundation had offered a grant of

$600,000 for a group of Mexican Americans to "do in urban areas what Cesar is doing in rural areas."

It was a start-up grant for the Southwest Council of La Raza (SCLR), which later became the National Council of La Raza. Although I wasn't ready to change my plans, the possibility of making a major difference for Mexican Americans in the Southwest intrigued me. After meeting with Henry and the new head of the SCLR, Herman Gallegos, I agreed to become director of research and information for this brand-new initiative in Phoenix.

The only staff supervisor besides Herman and me was a renegade priest named Miguel Barragan, who had just left the church because of a serious disagreement with his bishop over the Poor Peoples' March and was now out on his own. Little did I know how dramatically my life would soon be changed as I applied an earlier lesson: be a risk-taker—it can lead to some incredibly exciting life adventures. Exciting but also difficult.

Building an organization from scratch was exhilarating and challenging. Our small staff was committed to the "cause," loved what we were doing, and were convinced we would succeed. Swept up by the moment, we were involved in every initiative in the Southwest that focused on helping Mexican Americans. It often meant working around the clock to meet deadlines and crisscrossing the country for strategic meetings.

As the Chicano movement developed around us, one thing led to another, and I soon found myself falling in love with my co-worker Miguel. After two years of dating secretly, I decided that the relationship had to move toward marriage or I had to move on with my life. Under some duress, and not wanting to lose me, Miguel agreed to marry me if we could keep it a secret. He had not yet told his mother he had left the priesthood and was getting married. Foolishly, I agreed.

The marriage was doomed from the start, but it produced a beautiful little girl on June 16, 1971, whom we named Monica. A month later I left Miguel, returned to Denver, and found myself the subject of a major scandal. Despite sensational gossip about my torpedoed marriage and laments that I was dead politically, my family stood tall and supported me.

My political epitaph had been written. The word was that no young Mexican American woman could do what I had done and survive politically. I learned one of my hardest lessons: making mistakes and failing doesn't mean you're a failure. Only you can determine your success or failure.

When I left Miguel, I had no income and no job, only a determination to provide for my baby. Friends in Washington heard about my plight and offered me a job. Sobbing, I said, "Yes, but what do I do with my baby?" The answer was: "What's the movement all about if we can't help each other? Just bring the baby to the office. We'll figure it out."

Ethical Choices

Rick Bela and Raul Yzaguirre had started the first Chicano-owned and -operated consulting firm in Washington, D.C., called Interstate Research Associates, and had a three-month contract for me to staff. Before on-site child care, flextime, or alternative work schedules, I flew to Washington, baby in tow, to work on a flexible schedule. When I had to attend special meetings, staff members pitched in and looked after Monica.

Next I went to work for the Democratic National Committee (DNC), which was worried about Mexican Americans defecting to La Raza Unida, a new third party in the Southwest, and President Nixon's Chicano strategy to attract Mexican American voters.

I was hired as special assistant to DNC chairman Lawrence F. O' Brien, who knew me from the RFK campaign. He overlooked the criticism of some Chicano leaders that I was too young and inexperienced for such a critical position. My mother took care of

Monica during the eight-month assignment. The job required frequent travel in the Southwest, thus enabling me to spend weekends with Monica in Denver. But it made for crazy hours when I was in Washington.

After the 1972 Democratic convention, a new chair was elected who was unfamiliar with my work to consolidate Hispanic support. At her first staff meeting, Jean Westwood announced major changes that would have a negative impact on my efforts. I stormed out. I didn't realize that the man who followed me and inquired about my obvious displeasure was a reporter. When he identified himself, I asked not to be quoted, but the story appeared in the *Washington Post.*

The article produced calls from Jean Westwood and a concerned friend who worked for the Nixon White House. Despondent that my work was not appreciated, I agreed to a clandestine meeting with a couple of Hispanic Republicans. If I resigned and publicly stated displeasure with McGovern's lack of sensitivity to Hispanics, they suggested, I could choose one of two options: appointment as executive director of the U.S. Commission on Civil Rights or a $300,000 government contract to start a public relations business in Denver, plus a scholarship for my husband to go to law school, should we reconcile.

I confess it took a couple of days to say no. Someday I hoped to run for public office; I knew that anything a person does can always become public, even if it was once a secret. I didn't realize I had made an ethical decision that would positively affect the rest of my life. A year later, the offers made to me became public during the Watergate hearings. Fortunately I had declined!

Jean Westwood asked me to stay at the DNC, but I decided to go home, take care of my baby, and try to reconcile my marriage. Returning to Denver without a job was difficult. My entire network was based on contacts in the Democratic Party or Chicano movement, neither of which had any leverage in Colorado.

Every Person Counts

With savings, I bought a house and moved into a Democratic district in Adams County, where my parents, aunt and uncle, and ten sets of cousins lived (my main network). I took consultant jobs, volunteered to be my party's precinct committeewoman, and started organizing the Colorado Democratic Chicano Caucus.

Originally I planned to start small and run for city council. But my state representative decided to run for the state senate, and his most likely successor moved out of the district. That left an open seat; a Democratic vacancy committee would select the party's candidate. The committee comprised fifty-two precinct representatives, and eleven of the seats were unfilled.

When I expressed interest in the nomination, I was reminded that no woman or minority had ever been elected to a partisan office in the county's history. I was determined to change that. My supporters and I started recruiting people to run for the vacant precinct committee seats. In a district with fewer than 15 percent minority voters, we signed up two Native Americans, one Asian American, six Mexican Americans, and one Anglo woman to run as write-in candidates in the primary election. As it turned out, I needed every single one of those votes.

On the night the vacancy committee chose the Democratic party candidate, I defeated two other candidates by *one* vote. That's when I truly understood that every vote counts and, more important, that every person counts. I went door-to-door asking each voter for his or her vote and won with 69 percent of the vote.

I became the only Mexican American woman in the country to win a seat in a state house of representatives in November 1974 and was propelled into the national spotlight. But an even more significant event in my life was about to take place.

After my return to Colorado, Miguel agreed we should try to save our marriage. Unfortunately, the reconciliation was short-lived.

Immediately following my election, we had a serious disagreement, and he moved out of the house. Little did I know I had become pregnant. Later I was surprised at the number of people who advised me to abort the baby because of my political career.

I knew from the start I wanted this baby but wasn't sure how I was going to handle the situation while carrying out my role as a state representative. My estranged husband agreed not to say anything about our pending divorce until after the baby was born. To be the only Mexican American woman in the state legislature wasn't unusual enough; I had to be the first legislator to sit in session while pregnant!

I kept my pregnancy secret until it was impossible to hide, along about March. The larger I got, the more commotion I created in the legislature. The session usually ended in April or May, but the 1975 session turned out to be the longest in history. Concerned about suggestions I would not be able to fulfill my duties, I resolved not to miss any roll calls or committee meetings.

I kept getting bigger and bigger, and the session kept going on and on. Finally, on July 1 we voted to adjourn at 6 P.M.; my beautiful son showed great wisdom by choosing to be born the following day at 5:27 P.M. When he was nine days old, Miguelito went to his first meeting with the governor and Hispanic legislators, and a week later we started our full-day committee meetings.

A Spiritual Direction

Raising two children as a single mother and a member of the state legislature was a challenge, made easier by the support of my parents. The legislature met annually for only four to six months, and I supplemented my income with speaking fees. From January through May I worked long hours and saw little of my children during the week. On weekends they accompanied me to Democratic party fund-raisers, picnics, parades, dinners, seminars, conventions, and meetings.

I worried about my parenting skills and the lack of spiritual direction in my children's lives. I started looking for a church where Monica (now five years old) could go to catechism. Then it happened. I began serving on an advisory committee to the Adams County Mental Health Center, as did a new young priest, Father Charles J. Chaput.

I was captivated by Father Charles's understanding and sensitivity to the problems of ordinary folks. Sheepishly, I made an appointment to see him about joining his church. I felt it was important for him to understand my past failings and not allow anyone to hold my children accountable for my sins.

Father Chaput counseled me about my marriage to a priest and subsequent divorce, and assured me that God is very forgiving and has a great capacity for loving us imperfect human beings. I joined his church, which led to a strong bond of friendship between him and my family.

When Pope John Paul II made his first visit to the United States, President Jimmy Carter hosted a reception for him at the White House. As a member of the DNC executive committee, I invited Father Charles to attend the White House reception as my guest. I never imagined he would return the favor twenty years later. In June 1977, I was invited to attend the ceremony at the Vatican when Father Charles received his archbishop's pallium from Pope John Paul II, as the new archbishop for Northern Colorado.

My four years in the state house, eight years as the first minority woman in the state senate, and sixteen years as a member of the DNC were filled with excitement, challenge, and lots of strokes. For the first time in my life I was called "honorable" and treated with great deference as I traveled on study tours and speaking engagements, hobnobbing with some of the most important people in the world.

All along, my life lessons were constantly being challenged. Fortunately, I had learned first-hand about not prejudging, making good ethical decisions, and keeping a spiritual direction in my life. Those lessons served me well over two decades as I led a very public life in a goldfish bowl and raised two children with limited resources.

New Directions

Each life has many seasons, and my public life season was coming to an end. When I first ran for office, I believed I could change the way people treat Mexican Americans through the political process. I thought my mission was to be a role model and the first Hispanic woman member of Congress.

In 1980, I became the first Hispanic woman nominated by a major political party for the U.S. House of Representatives. I lost. But the election was a "free ride" because I was in the middle of my four-year state senate term. The following year, I was elected one of the DNC's three vice chairs. Among my supporters was a young DNC member from Arkansas who had lost his reelection bid for governor. In 1991, Bill Clinton asked me to return the favor.

In 1986, when Representative Tim Wirth announced he would leave the U.S. House of Representatives to run for the U.S. Senate seat vacated by Gary Hart, I decided to run again for Congress instead of seeking reelection to the state senate.

I lost the primary. The loss produced an overwhelming sense of rejection and tremendous feelings of guilt for not trying harder and disappointing so many people. My family suffered as well as my friends. It taught me that you need your full commitment, total effort, and complete heart to successfully tackle a new challenge.

I knew I had to replenish my energy and take care of my children. For the next three years, I operated my own consulting firm until becoming executive director of a new Hispanic institute sponsored by three inner-city colleges. In that position, I had a rare opportunity to develop a multicultural leadership development program called *Visiones*, which helped people better understand and work with one another and value cultural differences. I also enrolled in graduate school to earn a master's degree in public administration. But opportunity always has a way of changing my life.

In October 1991, I was called by a friend shortly after her husband announced his candidacy for president. Hillary Clinton asked me to co-chair Bill Clinton's campaign in Colorado. It was an exciting campaign that ended in victory on election day, the first time a Democrat had taken Colorado since 1964.

After the election, President Clinton appointed me as special assistant for consumer affairs and director of the U.S. Office of Consumer Affairs. By then my children, now eighteen and twenty-two years old, had made their own life decisions, which did not include moving to Washington. For the first time in twenty-two years, I was alone living without my children.

I began to take a hard look at what was really important in my life. It was *not* living in Washington and working at the White House without loved ones close by, even though I was proud to be part of the Clinton administration. The time had come to go home. Fortunately, an exciting position became available in Denver, and at the end of 1994, I became the regional administrator for the General Services Administration (GSA).

The Rocky Mountain Region had been designated a "reinvention region," which allowed for new, creative ways of managing government in a downsizing environment. Over a three-year period, with the assistance of consultants and a strategy of off-sites for both managers and support staff, we successfully addressed our behavior and attitudes in the workplace. The result was a series of employee-generated contracts addressing appropriate workplace behaviors for a healthy, happy, and productive work setting. I left GSA in June 1998 with a great deal of pride in the dramatic cultural change that the leadership team, managers, and support staff had achieved.

As I enter the final stage of my career, my primary focus is my spiritual growth and supporting the spiritual development of others.

Earning a six-figure income for five years financially enabled me to "retire" from government early. I am now CEO of my own consulting firm and a full-time volunteer for the Center for Contemplative Living, which is associated with St. Benedict's Monastery in Snowmass, Colorado, and Contemplative Outreach. The center is a spiritual network of individuals and small faith communities throughout the world, committed to renewing the contemplative dimension of the Gospel in everyday life.

I am still dedicated to my lifelong mission of helping people from diverse backgrounds value and appreciate one another and communicate more effectively, but now I am focused on the spiritual dimensions of that challenge. As I look back over my life, I am in awe of the God-given forces that allowed this shy Mexican American girl to experience such remarkable life adventures.

NEW DIRECTIONS

CELINDA C. LAKE is president of Lake Sosin Snell Perry and
Associates, a research-based strategy firm. She is one of the
nation's foremost experts on electing women candidates and
framing issues to women voters. As one of the Democratic
Party's leading political strategists, she has served as tactician
and senior adviser to party committees, incumbents, and chal-
lengers at all levels of the electoral process. She also has advised democratic parties in several Eastern European countries
and South Africa. Lake is a pollster for *U.S. News and World
Report*, former adviser to the *Wall Street Journal*, and author
of *Public Opinion Polling: A Manual for Public Interest
Groups* (1986). She holds a B.A. degree from Smith College
and an M.A. degree from the University of Michigan at Ann
Arbor.

What Do Women Want?

CELINDA C. LAKE

M Y FASCINATION WITH POLITICS started in Bozeman, Montana, where I grew up. My parents had moved from New York City to do the rather bohemian thing of owning a ranch in Montana. They were lifelong Republicans who encouraged me to think for myself. I remember them arguing over which candidate to support, especially the year mother wanted Rockefeller and my more conservative dad wanted Nixon. As a teenager I learned even more about GOP philosophy by attending Republican summer camp.

The West has been an extremely important influence on me. The tradition, especially in the agricultural West, is of equal partnership between women and men. It is a culture of opportunity and individualism as well as equal partnership. The West also has a heritage of strong women. Jeannette Rankin, the first woman ever to serve in Congress, was from Montana and was one of my childhood heroines.

I have a favorite photograph in my office that reminds me of my Montana roots and values. It's called "Cowgirls at the Roundup 1911" and shows a crowd of women all lined up on horses. The caption reads: "The emancipation of women may have begun, not with the vote, nor in the cities where women marched and carried signs and protested, but rather when they mounted a good cow horse and realized how different and fine the view. From the back of a horse the world looked wider."

Certainly there was plenty of sexism in the West as I was growing up; the crosscurrents of equality and sexism, and the conflict between the two, were catalytic in my life. My family was fairly traditional. My mother was a homemaker, and my father was rather conservative. I remember telling my dad that if I ever married I would not change my name. He was very upset about my feminism and "bra-burning" ideas until I explained that my decision meant I still wanted to be a Lake. He paused and said, "Oh, well, that is entirely different." Now we were talking about my individuality and my identity.

I fully recognized sex discrimination in high school when I wanted to run for student body president and was told: "Girls are not president; you have to run for secretary." Also, I was star of the girls' speech team, but that got me in trouble with the boys.

Once when a huge snowstorm kept people from getting to a competition, the boys' and girls' speech teams were merged. The guys had always liked me because I beat everyone else's girls. This time I not only beat the girls, I beat the boys, including the ones from my school. After that nobody would talk to me; nobody had warned me that I wasn't supposed to beat the boys.

I made up my mind to go to a women's college, because I knew women would hold all the top leadership positions. At the time, many traditional men's colleges had begun to open their doors to women. One was Yale, my father's alma mater, and I was very interested in the idea of becoming one of its first women students. But after the speech-team incident I thought, "Forget it, I'm going to a school where there are women only," and I chose Smith College.

From Montana to Massachusetts

I was a Republican, like my parents, until I switched to the Democratic Party after my junior year in college. I even ran a Students for Nixon group in Massachusetts. It was very small! I was one of the founders of Massachusetts Public Interest Research Group (PIRG), or Nader's Raiders as it was known then. The head of PIRG couldn't believe it. Here was this Republican from Montana who helped organize PIRG: "Who *are* you? Where did you *come* from?" he wanted to know.

Both the Vietnam War and the women's movement influenced me profoundly. They were equally important in changing the way I looked at the world; they challenged my thinking because they posed so many fundamental contradictions with what I knew to be real and what people were telling me.

Vietnam was very disorienting and complicated for me. I still have not completely sorted out my feelings about that war. Half of my high school classmates did not go to college, and lots of them were in Vietnam when I arrived at Smith in the fall of 1972.

Bozeman sat on the Canadian border, which was totally open. Anyone could have walked over to Canada; yet I never knew any people who did, or any "draft dodgers." It wasn't the ethic in my town to do such a thing. I remember being in tears and listening to the radio with my mother in the kitchen at home, as the lottery numbers for the draft were read and we waited for my brother's number to come up. There was no question that my brother would serve if his number was called.

I arrived in Massachusetts at the height of the antiwar movement. On my first day at Smith, students were organizing demonstrations and planning sit-ins at military bases. The only people who went to Vietnam, according to them, were "warmongers." I thought about all those guys from my high school class who were in Vietnam. I grew up with them; I knew them all my life. Even they didn't want to go to Vietnam, but where I came from nobody questioned going.

The Gender Gap

It wasn't until I took my junior year abroad that I learned about survey research. In Geneva, where I was studying, I found expatriate Americans from the University of Michigan who were doing comparative studies of voting behavior. Without a computer, I researched my first paper by using a card sorter with a punch card— and I loved it!

I planned to become an equal employment opportunity lawyer and had received early admission to Yale Law School. Once I discovered survey research, I changed my mind. The experience was very catalytic for me: I had always loved politics, but didn't realize you could actually do it as a profession.

In 1982, I began studying differences in women's and men's voting behavior for my master's thesis. What came to be known as the gender gap first emerged in the 1980s in response to the policies of President Reagan. Now, at the end of the 1990s, gender gap politics is key to national elections and the future of the Republican and Democratic Parties.

Even in Reagan's first presidential campaign, women were more uncertain about his priorities and policies than men. In 1986, the gender gap helped the Democrats win back control of the U.S. Senate. By the end of the 1980s, women systematically were identifying as Democrats over Republicans by four to eight percentage points and helped elect President Clinton in 1992.

In past elections, Democrats have won by generating strong support among women and narrowing the margin among men. Republicans have won by keeping the gender gap from becoming a gender canyon, targeting homemakers and religious conservatives among women and maximizing the enthusiasm of white men.

In the congressional elections of 1994, Democrats failed and Republicans succeeded. In the presidential election of 1996, the situation was reversed. President Clinton was reelected by the biggest gender gap in American political history: 54 percent of women chose him over candidate Bob Dole. Men, by contrast, almost tied their votes, with 44 percent for Dole and 43 percent for Clinton.

What is driving the women's vote? Issues. The underlying theme for women is economic security. Although women tend to be optimistic and personally resilient, they also are anxious about the economy and the economic future for their families. This anxiety crosses racial and class lines.

The three priority issues for women in the twenty-first century are education, retirement, and health care. For women, in particular, education is a huge issue; it is critical to their ability, and their children's, to succeed in a competitive and changing economy. And education is the key to independence and respect.

Our research shows women, more than men, filtering their political policy preferences through a focus on children and family. In fact, in 1996, married women voted overwhelmingly Democratic; married men split their votes evenly along party lines.

Women's economic worries differ from men's. Women worry most about unemployment and salaries and benefits, especially retirement and health care benefits. Men worry more about taxes and the deficit. Women believe a government safety net is important; men think the highest priority for government should be to provide opportunity for people.

In their struggle to make ends meet, women think of the economy in personal terms. Our surveys indicate they don't think they have a choice about working, and feel stretched for time. Both women and men think it is important for parents to spend more time with their children and teach them values. Many women express powerful dreams of owning their own small business as a way of combining work and family and of gaining more independence, flexibility, and control over their lives.

Ninety-nine percent of all American women will be in the paid workforce at some time in their lives. The scarcity of time for women has real implications for public policy and the kind of demands women place on employers. For women, flexible working hours are an extremely high priority. When we conduct focus groups with women and ask them how they combine and balance family and work, they reply emphatically that they juggle—they juggle like crazy. American women are engaged in a constant battle to keep all the balls in the air at the same time.

It's in the solutions to problems like these where men and women differ. Women challenge the orthodoxy that the economy is supreme and government is the problem, not the solution. Men still dream of small government or no government at all. Recent research indicates two-thirds of college-educated men think neither they nor their families will ever need a social net program; two-thirds of college-educated women, however, see themselves or their relatives needing government help. Men think it's a good day when government hasn't done anything bad to you!

What Do Women Want?

I'm often asked the age-old question, What do women want? The answer reminds me of a story from Montana. I returned there in 1982 as a lobbyist working to pass gender-free insurance. Montana was the first state, and remains one of the few states, to enact gender-free insurance. Having worked before in Montana state politics, I knew all the legislators, lobbyists, and party leaders.

The opposition was awesome; we were up against all kinds of money and the powerful insurance industry. Even so, we had mothers of legislators persuading them to switch their votes. Lobbyists on the other side became desperate; they couldn't figure out how these "girl lobbyists" were winning on the issue. Some of them approached a former boss of mine and asked, "What do the women want?" He told them, "I think they want exactly what they're asking for."

Until recently, women who voted differently from men tended to be single or widowed. Now married women are voting differently from their husbands. After the 1996 election, we found that 73 percent of married men thought their wives voted the same way they did; it turned out that only 49 percent of married women actually said they did.

As pollsters, we are beginning to observe the opinions of the first grown cohort of "latchkey" children. Young men between twenty-five and thirty-five years old, for example, are starting to influence changes in the workplace. Those who were home with siblings while their parents worked are demanding more family-friendly policies of their employers, such as parental leave, flexible hours, and on-site child care, so they can better balance work and family life. They had a great deal of responsibility in raising their brothers and sisters and are now very concerned about being involved with their own families.

Fathers of children under six resemble women in their voting patterns because they are more likely to vote for a political party that offers good family policies. Overall, both men and women are beginning to demand work and family arrangements that will enable them to balance both parts of their lives. But women continue to be ambivalent about working because it has not freed them from the notorious "second shift" at home.

Both the Democratic and Republican Parties now consider the gender gap a fairly permanent component in elections. The contest is over which party is more effective at targeting swing women voters, because they can determine the outcome of an election, even when they don't vote. In 1994, for example, a huge proportion of women who voted in the 1992 presidential election did not vote and helped swing Congress to the Republican party. Half of them returned for the 1996 presidential election and helped reelect President Clinton.

The Modern Campaign

My job as a pollster is to assist candidates in understanding the data our firm gathers on voting behavior so they can develop the kind of messages that will persuade voters. But the days are long gone when candidates could hope to educate voters en masse. Now a candidate must work within an environment where the average American family spends five minutes a week thinking about politics—and it's five minutes that family probably thinks are wasted.

At the same time, the coverage of serious issues by the electronic media has decreased drastically. The amount of air time a candidate gets on radio or television keeps shrinking with every election. The thirty-second sound bite of the late 1980s seemed too short then; now the average sound bite is about eight seconds.

None of these trends has enriched the quality of political debate, and it's not entirely the fault of politicians. It is partly a reflection of the time issue: at every election the public has a shorter attention span. It's also the result of a proliferation of television channels and a new generation of channel surfers who don't stay put very long. A television network used to be able to count on approximately twenty seconds to tell a viewer about a good idea; now it has to grab you while you're flicking from that network to ESPN or the weather channel.

So we advise our clients to downsize what they want to tell the voters. The way we explain this to a candidate is that he or she has to have one message, illustrated by no more than three things, and that's it. That's all you get to persuade a voter. We tell candidates to pretend they are standing in a supermarket by the dairy section when a shopper asks why they are running for office. They have one sentence to explain why, in between the selection of milk and the choice of butter. That's what politics is reduced to these days.

Repetition is critical, and the tiny sound bite is tossed over and over again to the audience. Although this sounds as though our politics is dumbed down so that no intelligent issues will ever be considered by the public, the good news is that people are interested in serious matters.

Our gender gap research indicates people do care about issues and are voting on the issues, and swing women voters and the twenty-five- to thirty-five-year-olds are beginning to change the political landscape. We will see their influence continue in the next century as they demand better education and health care, reduced military spending, and humane, activist government.

Women Pollsters

When I started my career in survey research, hardly any women were in the business. One of the first was Linda DiVall, who works for Republican candidates and is still one of my role models. Over the years Linda and I have made joint presentations on the women's vote and have watched the number of female pollsters dramatically increase since we both started in the business. Linda was one of the first women to own her own firm and gave me wonderful advice when I founded my company.

I think being a pollster is one of the best roles women can have in the world of political consulting. I tell young women trying to get into the business that the toughest job by far for women is to be a media consultant; it relies on proving you are personally powerful and persuasive with your ideas long before you can prove your expertise. Even today, most men in campaigns won't give women that kind of power. Politics in general is really tough for women, especially as consultants, because it relies on personal power. Power is not something we exercise comfortably and also not something people willingly grant us.

The great thing about polling is you have something technical to provide and you do it early in the process, so you can establish your credibility from the beginning. And the bottom line is, no matter how sexist the campaign, the operatives eventually have to ask you how to read the surveys. So sometimes I just sit and wait until I implicitly suggest to the campaign operatives, "When you decide to stop being like that, I'll tell you what my research means."

I was fortunate to begin my career at the same time women in the Democratic Party were emerging into many leadership positions. All the talk about "queen bee" women, how the first women aren't good to the ones who come after them, is not my experience at all. The first women were incredibly good to me and supportive. As I was breaking into polling, a lot of women were also beginning to manage campaigns. They said, "OK, guys, there is one pollsterette we're going to interview along with the others"; they would almost bodily insert themselves in the door to keep it from closing.

One of the best jobs I ever had was working for the Women's Campaign Fund in 1986. It provided me an incredible network of women candidates and political operatives who to this day give me the strongest help and support in my business. Going out on my own in 1995 was one of the biggest risks I have ever taken, but someday I may look back on the founding of my own firm as a fundamental turning point in my career.

My goal for the nation's future is that public policy will become dominated by the values of tolerance and opportunity for all people. By the time I retire, my wish is for half the Congress to consist of women and people of color. But first I want to help elect the first woman president. I want to be her pollster.

ANGELA E. OH is a Los Angeles–based attorney and member of the Advisory Board to the President's Initiative on Race. She is a leader in bar and civic organizations. Following the 1992 riots in Los Angeles, the state legislature appointed her as special counsel to the Assembly Special Committee on the Los Angeles Crisis. She is a member of the Los Angeles City Human Relations Commission, past president of the Korean Bar Association of Southern California, and she served on the board of the California Women's Law Center. From 1995 to 1997 she was lawyer representative to the Ninth Circuit Judicial Conference. Oh holds B.A., M.P.H., and J.D. degrees from the University of California at Davis.

Beyond Self-Interest

ANGELA E. OH

A S A VERY YOUNG CHILD, I was fortunate to have been raised by my mother's mother. I never knew her by any name except *Halmoni,* Grandmother. As my parents completed their undergraduate studies and took odd jobs to help make ends meet, I spent my days and nights with my *wei-halmoni* (my mother's mother), whose living room area was crammed with card tables and strips of silk material.

The card tables filled up in the evenings with students who brought groceries that my grandmother would turn into "home-cooked" Korean meals (her kitchen was probably the first Korean restaurant in Los Angeles). The silks would eventually be sewn into men's ties, handkerchiefs, and pocket linings to be sold somewhere in the garment district in Los Angeles. My grandmother's rented house on the corner of Jefferson and Vermont was a meeting place where visitors were constantly coming and going. One day, even a Miss Korea appeared at my *halmoni*'s home. That was sometime in 1956 or 1957.

My grandmother was a passionate, fiercely independent, and courageous woman who barely spoke enough of the English language to communicate beyond "Hello. How are you?" "Thank you," and "Please, eat." Smiles, facial expressions, gestures, and sheer enthusiasm over meeting a new, friendly face were the ways that permitted her to get to know people, despite the language barrier. Her ability to communicate without words and her creativity of expression would allow non-Korean speakers to "converse" with her for many hours over a meal or an afternoon spent together.

Only as a college student did I realize that she had made a decision to leave everything behind in Seoul, Korea, at the age of sixty for a singular reason—to raise her youngest daughter's first child, me. My *halmoni* left me with a gift that I now recognize as the source of my being.

Today, I find myself engaged in a task that requires me to call upon the strength and insight an individual derives from having received the gift of unconditional love as part of her early childhood. It is a clarity of vision about who I am and the consistency of values that I have come to possess that allow me to know how to fulfill a very challenging and public duty I have agreed to accept on behalf of the American people. That duty is to serve as one of seven advisers to the president of this nation, as he leads the country in an unprecedented effort to begin a conversation about race, racism, and the possibility of racial reconciliation in America.

On June 14, 1997, President Clinton appeared before an audience of faculty, graduates, and their friends and families at the University of California in San Diego to deliver a commencement message, "One America in the Twenty-First Century." He celebrated the achievements of the new graduates, acknowledged the hard work and dedication of the faculty, families, and friends of the class of 1997, and challenged all of America to recognize that we stand at a crossroads. More specifically, he asked that we consider the question of our future as a nation. Will America choose to pursue a path of inclusion and fulfill the promise of equality and justice for all of its people, or will we fall prey to the temptation to pursue self-interest and the politics of division and exclusion as we move into the next century?

As President Clinton spoke, he reflected upon the successes of his administration in its efforts to respond to some of the most delicate, complex issues concerning the economy, politics, and international relations. He also noted, however, that one of the most deeply disturbing and persistent problems at home is that we continue to struggle with racial prejudice, misunderstanding, and paralysis in overcoming the obstacles presented by racial divides.

In announcing his Initiative on Race in the absence of any political, economic, or social crisis, the president expressed a clear understanding that overcoming chasms caused by racial prejudice is essential in maintaining our ability to move forward and prosper as a nation.

A New Paradigm

In my role as one of seven advisers on the bipartisan advisory board, I have urged that the study, dialogue, and action directed at race relations take place within a paradigm that is inclusive of those who are neither black nor white. The proposition that we move to a more inclusive paradigm in the discussion of race relations in America spurred an enormous amount of discussion in the press and in academic circles.

The suggestion that the new paradigm must seek to include people who are neither black nor white apparently represented a genuine and serious threat to those who have built their careers, reputations, and organizations around the white-black analysis. In light of the demographic trends in the country, it is clear that in order for any paradigm to have continuing relevance in the area of race relations over the next century, an expanded and more inclusive set of principles must emerge.

At one of the early meetings of the full advisory board, we reviewed demographic data confirming that significant changes will take place over the next fifty years. If current birth and immigration patterns persist, the racial composition of America by the year 2050 will shift dramatically in several instances: Hispanics will reach about 25 to 26 percent of the population, Asians will reach about 8 percent, African Americans will remain constant at about 14 percent, and non-Hispanic whites will be about 51 percent.

The reality of a "new majority" is reflected already in the current composition of Los Angeles County, with Hispanics at 43.5 percent of the population, African Americans at 9.9 percent, Asian Americans at 11.4 percent, and non-Hispanic whites at 35.1 percent.

Proposing a more inclusive race paradigm is not equivalent to suggesting that the black-white chasm should not continue to be examined and remain central to the developing discourse. Indeed, particular attention *must* continue to be paid to the dynamics that occur within that part of the discussion on race relations, because the strongest public attention and reaction occurs in situations in which the black-white chasm comes into play.

More important, our failure as a nation to deal directly with questions of justice and equality are most dramatically illustrated when we examine the data that describe the state of African Americans (and especially young adult males) when it comes to questions concerning the quality of life as measured by health, education, housing, criminal justice statistics, and employment. Thus the continued focus on the black-white dynamic is necessary, but not sufficient, to inform adequately and to address the problem of race, racism, and reconciliation in America as we enter the next century.

In considering what the twenty-first century paradigm might offer, it is vital to recognize that there must be serious consideration given first to gathering basic facts. The information foundation for the emerging paradigm must include multiracial or biracial Americans, Native Indian Americans, Latinos and Hispanics, Native Americans of the Pacific Islands, and Asian Americans. There exist unique expressions of racism, experiences with inter- and intragroup bigotry and prejudice, unprecedented complexities related to generational differences, influences that are based upon cultural expectations, customs, and practices, and (not surprisingly) resolution of some of the most confounding problems created by racial divides.

Out of a desire to contribute to the ultimate goal of moving beyond self-interest to create a society that reflects principles of justice and equality of opportunity, a thoughtful new generation of voices is joining the discussion on race and the advocacy efforts directed at improving not only race relations but also how a democracy functions when diverse interests are at play. Those who traditionally have been ignored in the study and discussion concerning race relations in America are now informing the whole about experiences that must be recognized, documented, and analyzed.

The particular ways in which this new information may be synthesized is endless. Policy experts, economists, social scientists, health experts, business interests, political strategists, spiritual leaders, community activists, and many others will find that the data being gathered will provide new opportunities to build mutually beneficial relationships.

The "Model Minority"

One of the challenges for Asian Pacific Americans will be to examine the peculiarity of being in a position of "simultaneity." In describing the concept of simultaneity, professor of law Eric Yamamoto, of the University of Hawaii, asserts that Asian Pacific Americans occupy the dubious distinction of being the "model minority," the "model victim," the "model mascot" in the current discourse on race relations.

At the same time, we are considered perpetrators of oppression upon other minorities, including African Americans, Hispanics, and Latinos. In the eyes of non-Hispanic whites, we are the "good minority." In the eyes of others, including African Americans and Hispanics and Latinos, we are the "honorary" whites.

Internally, Asian Pacific Americans feel the pressure of being the "wedge minority." How we respond to issues of the day, especially those issues that implicate principles of equality, justice, and fundamental notions of decency and fairness, will define the place we, as a community of color, will occupy in American culture and history.

The model minority concept emerged in the 1960s. It suggests that Asian Americans are superminorities, who enjoy success and acceptance by mainstream society because of a willingness to work hard and an ability to achieve in academics. The concept is considered mythical because the "data" used to support the claim that Asian Pacific Americans are superachievers are flawed.

For example, in describing economic status, "household" incomes are often used. Consideration is never given to the fact that income figures reported are based on several individuals contributing to a single household. Nor do the income data explain that Asian Pacific Americans are concentrated in regions of the country where the cost of living is higher, so that, in general, all incomes in the regions where they live are higher than the national average.

In times of social, cultural, and political contraction, such as the times in which we find ourselves today, it is essential for core values possessed by Americans of Asian and Pacific Islander ancestry to be asserted. In November 1996, when California voters were asked to eliminate affirmative action by voting for Proposition 209, proponents targeted Asian Pacific Americans as the poster children against affirmative action. Our vote showed that we can move beyond self-interest; an overwhelming majority of Asian Pacific American voters rejected Proposition 209. A *Los Angeles Times* poll indicated that

61 percent of Asian Americans voted no on proposition 209; the Asian Pacific American Legal Center (APALC) poll indicated 76 percent rejected it.

This outcome came in spite of organizers who sought to promote the initiative among Asian Pacific Americans by constantly appealing to their perceived selfishness, arguing that Asian children would benefit by gaining a larger share of academic admissions if affirmative action were eliminated.

For those who engaged in thoughtful and informed consideration of the measure, it was readily apparent that our long-term goal to help build a society that strives to make equality a reality meant that we would need to shoulder some of the burden for reaching that goal.

The Case of Bill Lann Lee

The political price for taking that position was high. In the fall of 1997, Bill Lann Lee paid the price. A civil rights attorney with twenty-three years of experience litigating on behalf of plaintiffs who had suffered discrimination in employment, Lee was nominated to serve as the highest ranking official in the Department of Justice, responsible for enforcing federal civil rights laws. In the course of his nomination and confirmation process, extraordinary consideration was given to evaluating his credentials, his legal experience, and his personal background.

At the age of forty-five, Lee had gained ample experience in his field. He would instantly have commanded the respect of his trial lawyers within the Department of Justice because all of them would have known that he had spent the last twenty-three years of his career seeking to enforce the civil rights laws on behalf of his clients in our courts.

No better candidate could have emerged to lead the agency in fulfilling its role on behalf of the American people. Yet because of his job as regional director at the NAACP Legal Defense Fund (one of a few places where an attorney could actually make a career out of litigating civil rights cases), Republican senator Orrin Hatch of Utah and conservative Republican activists led by Clint Bolick of the Institute for [In]Justice vowed to impede the confirmation of Bill Lann Lee.

There is no doubt that the opposition to Lee was based on one issue: Proposition 209. What is tragic about this particular scenario is that Lee's opponents tried to deprive the American people of the opportunity to count among its national leadership an exceptional individual of Asian descent whose contribution to the field of civil rights would help lead us all beyond the black-white paradigm.

Overcoming Self-Interest

As the process continues, Asian Pacific Americans, along with all Americans, will need to consider the question as to whether self-interest can be overcome in order to build a community of justice. This means that all racial groups will need to examine shortcomings from within the community, considering where prejudice and bias end and individual responsibility begins, and whether opportunities to collaborate will be taken up or ignored.

I have often said that the notion that only one "pie" exists from which each of us may take "a piece" is as deceptive as it is stifling. But in keeping with the analogy, I believe that in establishing mutually beneficial relationships, there will be ways to expand the options, indeed, bake more pies (even if we have to work overtime).

Our nation's human resources have been largely untapped when it comes to examining the question of how diverse groups of people might find a shared sense of identity as Americans. There is a pressing need to unify the country. This is so because America stands as one nation among many, competing in a world economy, seeking to maintain and even increase its global economic and political standing, and striving to maintain a democracy that many other countries around the world are trying to replicate.

All of what we do is affected by the capacity of all interested parties (both domestic and international) to transmit information and images at an unprecedented speed. If we are to continue to occupy a position of leadership in the world, we must be clear about our fundamental principles and our commitment to them. We have been offered an opportunity to discuss and to decide upon the core values that we wish to embrace as we examine the question of race, racism, and reconciliation. The journey led by the president is a very public one in which the core values of respect and dignity must be maintained.

Moreover, there is no doubt that each of us must also undertake a very private journey as well. In taking that individual journey, we can only hope that the doubts that are so deeply ingrained in our experiences can be loosened and washed away by the thoughtful, constructive dialogue that emerges from the Initiative on Race. In the end, we will understand that the effort is truly a most remarkable endeavor to reach people's hearts.

MARIA HINOJOSA is CNN correspondent, author, and host of National Public Radio's *Latino USA*. Before joining CNN, she spent six years at NPR as a New York–based general assignment correspondent and also hosted *Visiones* on WNBC-TV in New York. She is the author of *Crews: Gang Members Talk with Maria Hinojosa* (1995). Her forthcoming book is a motherhood memoir about raising a Latino child in a multicultural society. In 1995, *Hispanic Business* magazine named her one of the one hundred most influential Latinos in the United States, and she won the Robert F. Kennedy award for her NPR story "Manhood Behind Bars." She holds a B.A. degree from Barnard College.

"My Otherness" is based on a telephone interview with Maria Hinojosa and on her speeches.

My Otherness

❦

MARIA HINOJOSA

AT THE AGE OF SIX I realized for the first time I was "different" and that my difference could have dire consequences for me and my family in America. It was 1968, and George Wallace was running for president. As I was walking down the street one day with a Jewish friend, we started making plans about where to hide if Wallace won. We were certain that he wanted to kill people like us.

About that time I also was hearing American leaders who spoke to me as an "American." Martin Luther King Jr. and Cesar Chavez are the two I remember. They made me feel there was a reason I was in this country—because people like them were also here.

I was born in Mexico City and grew up in Chicago. We moved to the United States when I was a year old because my father, a research physician, took a job at the University of Chicago. Periodically we returned to *la patria* to visit relatives. *Como Mexico no hay dos,* "like Mexico there is no other," was the phrase I often heard as our family of six piled into our station wagon and drove from Chicago to Mexico.

Soon I came to understand that in both places I was considered the "other": Mexican by Americans in the United States and American by my relatives in Mexico. As unsettling as it seemed to me then, the concept of not fitting into any category is something I now live with and embrace.

A Voice of the Voiceless

I will never forget the day in high school when I was in my room playing with the FM radio dial and found a news program in Spanish called *Enfoque* on National Public Radio (NPR). The reporters were speaking in complete sentences, and no disk jockeys were yelling into the mikes. It fulfilled me to hear news about Latin America, seriously and professionally done. I knew I would end up working there one day.

In 1979, I entered Barnard College in New York City, intending to become an actress and dancer. But soon I was pulled toward radio and began hosting a Spanish language program on the college station.

When National Public Radio hired me in 1985, I became the first Latina to work in its Washington, D.C., headquarters. What an honor it was a year later when I was hired in San Diego as the producer of *Enfoque,* the same show that had made such an impression on me as a teenager!

I was living again in New York City and working as an NPR reporter when, in the fall of 1990, Brian Watkins, a young tourist from Utah, was stabbed to death as he tried to defend his family from a subway mugging. He was murdered by a member of a gang who, it turned out, wanted money to go dancing.

NPR assigned me to investigate New York gangs, or "crews," and I began to ask, listen, and learn. Like many others, I had a hard time understanding what made it so easy for a teen to reach into his pocket, pull out a knife, and stab someone.

My ten-minute documentary, "Crews," was a harsh, graphic, telling account of juveniles discussing violence as a means of getting power and recognition. It also provoked an angry reaction from NPR listeners who were upset that gang members were getting airtime.

For two years I pursued this story after I decided to write a book about it, hanging out in neighborhoods and schoolyards to gain the trust of crew members; boys, girls, white, black, and Latino. I reported on crews that had replaced the family for their members as the members' primary support system. When they didn't want to or couldn't go home, they tried to create a family on the streets.

All of them had a difficult time communicating with their parents, and many of them were physically abused, starting in early childhood. They were surrounded by violence and social and economic barriers that to them appeared insurmountable. They joined crews to get respect and power and to be valued. One boy told me that by listening to them I earned their respect "because you showed us respect. We don't like people who are afraid of us. We're not that bad; we just want recognition."

As much as we disapprove of young people like these, they are part of our society and our responsibility. My reporting was not meant to be a solution to the problem; it was a way for these youths to speak their minds so we can understand how to help them and ourselves. Given a chance, many of them could end up as good people. Their lives are savable if we want to save them.

Trusting My Voice

As a Latino woman and journalist I have struggled to trust my voice. When you grow up as a person of color in this country, you constantly are told there is something wrong with what you are thinking. I have been described variously as a reporter with an agenda, someone with an ax to grind, or a cute little "Chiquita Banana." So it has been a tremendous effort getting to the point where I not only trust my voice, I also trust what my experience is telling me.

My biggest challenge growing up was coming to terms with my identity. I even hated my name for a long time because I thought it emphasized my difference. Now I like my name; it is me. As a child I always felt voiceless; as a reporter I try to capture the voices of the other and bring them into the mainstream media. I try to uncover a side of America that we usually don't hear from.

I document the lives of people I see day in and day out, people whom editors, managing editors, bureau chiefs, and vice presidents don't see because of their lifestyles and history. That's not to say my way is better. It's a recognition of the difference, and the importance of bringing that difference into the media. We all have American experiences and American voices that need to be heard and documented.

When Mother Teresa died, for example, I did a remembrance through the eyes of people in the South Bronx where her mission is located. We talked to young African American men who appear to be just "guys in the 'hood" but who are very religious, very committed, and dedicated to the memory of Mother Teresa. I interviewed a Puerto Rican teenager who is devoting her life to counseling young drug-addicted teens, and a mother whose daughter was blessed by Mother Teresa.

That is what I do: I put people on the air whom most of us would never imagine to be tied to someone like Mother Teresa, and give them a voice. Most of them have no voice, ever.

We in the news media foster the image of young men of color as criminals. Immediately following the Oklahoma City bombing, I was assigned to look into initial allegations of a Middle Eastern Muslim connection. Soon it became apparent that the prime suspect was Timothy McVeigh, who responded to accusations about his involvement by asking, "Do I look like a criminal?"

I think we know what Timothy McVeigh thinks criminals look like. The person responsible for the greatest act of terrorism in U.S. history was neither a young man of color nor an Arab immigrant. He was America's image of the "boy next door." The lesson of Oklahoma City is that we must no longer see the enemy as the person who looks the most unlike us.

Once after I aired a story on heroin use in the South Bronx, a colleague at NPR asked, "Aren't you nervous going into those neighborhoods? Aren't they scary and horrible?" I said, "No, I live in those neighborhoods." She didn't think to ask me how I felt coming to NPR as the first Latina. That was much scarier for me.

When journalists report on people whom the press tend to ignore or treat unfairly, they are helping to change the world. But they don't always tell the whole story or tell it accurately.

It happened to me one morning when I was on maternity leave and not working. I woke up to the sounds of gunshots. I didn't grow up hearing those sounds, but they have become customary. Now I can identify gunshots; I can tell whether or not they are coming from an automatic weapon.

I went into a panic because I realized my husband was outside with our two-month-old son. It was a moment of absolute, excruciating fear. They were fine, but a nine-year-old boy was shot in the shoulder, caught in the middle of a drug turf war.

Immediately after the shooting, a lot of journalists descended on my neighborhood. I expected them to parachute in, file a story on this one incident, and leave with that as their image of the community. They didn't know that a year before there were no drugs; the area had been abandoned and allowed to become a drug market by the authorities. As far as they were concerned, this was a poor neighborhood filled with people who were part and parcel of the drug trade. Nothing could be further from the truth.

I had so many mixed feelings. I, too, have been a parachute reporter, covering breaking news without having the time ever to explore the depth and complexity of a community, the shifting of power, and why certain things result. But this time it took place right in front of my house.

A Real American Holiday

When I first moved to New York City in 1979, I suffered culture shock. Between Anglo Chicago or Mexican Chicago I could find my place. But New York was something else—no place to find real tortillas; where were the chilis? There weren't many Mexicans, so I became a Pan Latin–Americanist and began to socialize with Peruvians, Dominicans, Puerto Ricans, and others. Since then the Mexican community has exploded.

Now there are enough Mexicans in New York that each year on November 1 and 2 we observe the Day of the Dead. The celebration has grown in one decade from a single parade to public events all over the city. I hope the Day of the Dead will become a real New York City American holiday. That will establish the Mexican community as a part of our city and also educate other New Yorkers about the traditions of their neighbors.

The Day of the Dead marks the time of year Mexicans believe the souls of the dead return to earth. In Mexico, cemetery plots are cleaned; people build altars and spend nights at the graves of their loved ones, which are covered with flowers. Altars contain family mementos, sugar skeletons, candles to help the souls find their way, and water to quench their thirst on the long journey back to earth.

In New York we can't build altars in cemeteries, so they are usually built in homes. It's a spontaneous, creative, organic process that takes shape in the space you are using. Since 1990, I have built altars with my artist husband, German Perez, including ones dedicated to the memory of immigrants who died crossing the border, people who died of AIDS, and young victims of police brutality. Each altar responds to its moment in history, keeping a tradition alive that is changing as it blends Mexican and American customs.

The Day of the Dead is a celebration of life, of memory, and of people who have been lost. The souls of the dead are very much alive, and we confront rather than fear death, which is a natural part of every person's life.

Embracing the Other

In 1989, I finally acknowledged that I am always going to live in the United States and will never again live in Mexico City. I needed to take responsibility for my own activism, become part of this country, and exercise my right to vote.

Having a Mexican passport was very important to me, but my husband and I understand that we and our American-born children are Latino citizens of this country who are not from "back there." This is our homeland.

In their own lives our children will grow up with diversity. With a Dominican-born father and Mexican-born mother, they are a combination of two Latin American cultures, being raised in a mixed African American and Latino community. I think the experience of integrating the many parts of who they are is going to be very organic, as it was for me—even though I grew up with a lot of self-hatred, which I hope they can avoid.

I want my children to develop an appreciation of their cultural identity without its becoming the central focus of their lives. At the same time, they need to own their American-ness, which is something I didn't do; I always felt I was the other.

Unfortunately, twenty years from now when they are in college, they probably will still have the sense of being a "minority." The way we use the term minority, defined as "less than," perpetuates barriers in this nation. To borrow from author Sandra Cisneros, I define multiculturalism as being able to see yourself in the person who is most unlike you. It means finding the humanity in the person we think has none.

No group at this point in our history can claim to be superior or to own the American experience or to believe there is only one type of American experience. We are all the other and need to recognize our own otherness. The other is not something for us to deny but rather to embrace, for it is the equalizing element that brings us together in this nation.

A Lifeline

Journalists like me have the cameras and microphones that can be the lifeline to people who are excluded. It happened to John Guardo. Moments before I first met John he had been released from a police lineup. It was hard to believe this boy could frighten men twice his age and size, but he could.

In my documentary "Crews," John talked about beating white men but also mentioned his dream of becoming an engineer or a lawyer. That interview was the lifeline that helped him leave his crew, get a job, and become a commentator on *Latino USA*.

When the National Association of Hispanic Journalists gave "Crews" its award in 1990, I took John to the ceremony. As we accepted the award, he nervously took the microphone and began to speak. John told a stunned audience that listening to his own voice on the radio had changed his life: "I heard myself say that I was going to amount to something, and I believed me."

My otherness has always made me want to give a voice to the voiceless. I have grown to understand that my way of seeing the world is as valid as anyone else's. But if I don't touch people with my reporting, I am not doing my job.

AMY R. SIMON is vice president of the public opinion research firm, Bennett, Petts, and Blumenthal. From 1996 to 1997, she was political director of the National Jewish Democratic Council and from 1993 to 1996 was political director of the Women's Campaign Fund and program director of the Women's Campaign Research Fund. Formerly she was vice president of the November Group, a persuasion mail firm where she was a communications strategist for nonprofit organizations, labor unions, and political campaigns. Simon was an organizer in the 1988 Dukakis presidential campaign and a co-founder of the Women's Information Network, which named her its Young Woman of Achievement for 1994. She holds a B.A. degree from the University of Michigan.

Getting Political

AMY R. SIMON

I GREW UP in a middle-class family with a mother who stayed home to raise the children and a father who worked to support the family. Though she did not work for pay, my mother was a committed conservationist and environmentalist who shared with my brother and me her love for the splendor and beauty of the natural world and her commitment to preserve it. She developed an educational curriculum for elementary school students, coauthored a book on Native American Indian habitats, and created beautiful art made of twigs, plants, flowers, and seashells that filled our life in the Boston suburb of Wayland and our vacations on Cape Cod.

My mother was a famously stubborn woman who fought intense battles to protect her family, friends, and the issues that concerned her. Her example and her unqualified support taught me it is important to stand up for what you believe, even if your actions make someone else angry.

My mother died young, at forty-two. She first had breast cancer when she was only thirty-nine, and had a radical mastectomy. Survival rates in the 1970s were even worse than they are today. The chances of her living more than five years were fairly small, and the possibility of her dying was not something she shared with me at the time.

I remember her being sick and going into the hospital for surgery, and seeing the long, long line of angry black stitches where her breast had been. She explained to me that the stitches were not permanent, that they would come out and then she would be fine. From my child's eye, she was fine, and for a while life hummed along as it had before.

I was ten years old when the breast cancer came back, and for nine long months she fought its debilitating effects. Walking in the woods surrounding our house was a solace for her, and she always lit up when I brought her shells, rocks, or flowers from my own wanderings. I remember her crying bitterly when she was given a wheelchair because the cancer had spread to her bones and she could no longer walk in the woods and fields.

Knowing she was dying, she talked to me about her life in ways one ordinarily might not share with a girl only eleven years old: her proudest moments, her painful choices, and even some of her regrets. Even now I am both astounded and grateful that she was willing to discuss such adult subjects with me. Whether or not I was ready, she knew this was my only chance to learn about her life from her, rather than through the point of view of her friends and family later on.

Although there are countless ways in which my mother's life shaped mine, one of the most dramatic was my so-early-in-life realization that one could die, with no second chances, feeling unfulfilled, seeing wasted opportunities, and regretting choices you had made.

This is not to suggest my mother was on balance unhappy with her choices—to the contrary, she was quite proud of her family and her contributions to the community.

I took upon myself an awesome task as she lay dying—don't waste a day, not even a moment of a day. Live fully, experience everything, see the world, learn about other people, try to make the world a better place, and never regret a choice once made. I couldn't imagine anything worse than lying on my own deathbed filled with regrets. So I became determined to live without any. Not that I wouldn't make mistakes—I wouldn't regret them. Mistakes were a part of learning and living life fully. This commitment to myself has been both a great gift and a great burden.

Organizing

Although I love learning and intellectual exploration, I have always needed to be "doing" as well. My first experience with political organizing was spurred by a speech at my high school given by Dr. Helen Caldecott, founder of Physicians for Social Responsibility. She showed us declassified black-and-white slides taken by the U.S. military, documenting the effects of the nuclear blasts and radiation in the few weeks immediately following the bombing of Hiroshima and Nagasaki. The photos were so disgusting and vivid, I actually became nauseated.

Many other students were upset, so we formed an organization for high school students to oppose nuclear weapons and planned an all-day teach-in at school. That experience was incredibly empowering—as teenagers we not only arranged a major event, we also invited nationally prominent speakers, and they came!

We soon joined private high school students in starting the Newton North High School chapter of Student-Teacher Organization to

Prevent Nuclear War (STOP Nuclear War). I joined the STOP national board of directors, where I met a wonderful student organizer, Vanessa Kirsch, who like many others in my world of social change, kept reappearing in my life.

STOP was an incredible training ground for us. Fortunately, we were surrounded by adults who gave us tremendous support, patiently guiding our ideas and dreams without taking them over. We learned how to organize for social change, raise funds, conduct petition drives, and lobby. Most important, we learned that by joining together we could make the world a better place.

In June 1982, we organized five busloads of students to attend a massive Central Park rally against nuclear war. When it was time to sign the contract for the buses, I was told you had to be eighteen to sign. I was offended and thought it silly—I had raised the money to pay the bus company, why shouldn't I sign?

We conducted a nationwide petition drive, collected fifteen thousand student signatures, and organized a lobbying trip to present the petitions to Congress. In June 1983, busloads of high school students from five separate states arrived in Washington, D.C., just as Congress was to begin voting on the nuclear freeze. Of course, we were a public relations dream for the pro-freeze side. Congressman Ed Markey (Democrat, Massachusetts) and Senator Ted Kennedy (Democrat, Massachusetts) recognized the potential and assigned staff people to help us. We wandered the halls of Congress, delivering petitions and talking to staff and members of Congress on the importance of a nuclear freeze for our future.

That fall when I entered the University of Michigan, I was already a little burnt out on politics and decided to take a break and focus on my studies. Little did I realize how much the social action bug had bitten me. By the second semester, I already was involved with the Public Interest Research Group in Michigan (PIRGIM), working on traditional PIRG issues like toxic waste cleanup.

When a male PIRGIM staffer called attention to my own use of sexist language, it was truly a "eureka" experience for me. I began to view sexism in a new light, seeing its insidious impact in everyday ways I had never before appreciated. So a group of us began the PIRGIM Women's Issues Committee and organized multiple campus educational programs on issues of sexism and racism.

While my views of feminism were beginning to take shape, I experienced firsthand an issue facing all women: personal safety. One night I was attacked walking on campus with a friend. Although I got away and was not physically harmed, the attack terrified me and disempowered me in profound ways. That assault is most likely what drove me in 1985 to help found a program called SAFEWALK, a nighttime walking program using student-trained volunteers.

It was in the summer of 1986 that I became a Democrat. I interned at the bipartisan Congressional Caucus for Women's Issues, co-chaired by Congresswomen Pat Schroeder (Democrat, Colorado) and Olympia Snowe (Republican, Maine). I was then a registered Independent, believing both the Republican and Democratic Parties were establishment sellouts and could not represent my beliefs.

My views changed dramatically while working on Capitol Hill, following legislation, and seeing how slow and hard it was to make change. I concluded that to be effective at that level you must engage from the inside—either as a Democrat or a Republican. Listening to the views of the Republicans on Capitol Hill, I knew I wasn't a Republican, so I became a Democrat, an affiliation I expect to be lifelong.

Busy as I was with organizing, I struggled to decide "what to do when I grow up." Graduate school did not look like a decision, only a means of delaying one. I did not grasp that an entire world exists of professional social and political activists who earn a decent living making the world a better place. Somewhat at a loss, I decided to go into business and work for social change as an avocation rather than a vocation. After graduation in June 1987, I took a business job in Boston, intending to stay for several years.

Campaigning

In the summer of 1987, the field of Democratic presidential candidates comprised eight hopefuls—dubbed "Snow White and the Seven Dwarfs" by the press—and I decided to throw my hat in with Snow White (a.k.a. Pat Schroeder). I worked at a house party to raise money for her campaign, cried when she dropped out, and became enraged at the sniping over Schroeder's tears when she announced her withdrawal. Disgruntled as I was, I looked at the remaining candidates and picked my new horse, hometown candidate Michael Dukakis.

I had no political connections and didn't even understand they would help. When I asked about a job on the Dukakis campaign, I was told that only after volunteering full-time for three or four months would I even be considered for a job! Disappointed and seeing no way to eat or pay rent as a full-time volunteer, I settled into my business job.

In December I got a call from an old high school friend and STOP Nuclear War organizing buddy who was working for Dukakis in Des Moines. They needed volunteers for two weeks preceding the Iowa caucuses and would pay airfare and provide housing. I sent in my resume, excited about this potential opportunity and willing to spend my two weeks of annual vacation in Iowa in January.

Then Jill Alper from the campaign called—they didn't want me for the volunteer program, they wanted to hire me! The job paid $100 per week with no health benefits and would last five weeks until the Iowa caucuses. I asked my boss for a month-long leave of absence, which she (understandably) denied. After twenty-four hours and many thoughts about my mother's life regrets, I quit my job and flew to Des Moines, thinking I would simply find new work when I returned to Boston in February.

My experience in Iowa was profound and overwhelming and exciting and unbelievable all at once. The Iowa state director for Dukakis, Teresa Vilmain, ran the campaign headquarters like a boot camp, but appreciating her staff's youth, made it a bit like summer camp as well. Two of us shared a one-room apartment, and having no car, we walked the half mile to work in the bitter cold weather when we couldn't bum a ride. We worked from 10 A.M. until 1:00 A.M. every day except Sunday, when we were allowed to come in at noon. Like in summer camp, I was pleased to reconnect with such old organizing buddies as Vanessa Kirsch, who was stationed in Ames.

After the Iowa caucuses, a carload of us drove to Hibbing, Minnesota, to work in the heavily Democratic Iron Range. The campaign life was never easy, and it was often downright brutal. We were young, inexperienced staff people in over our heads, needing to make miracles happen on no sleep and with no money and succeeding a surprising amount of the time. As the primary season progressed and fewer states remained, the campaign regularly cut extra field staff to save money. After every primary, having worked fifteen to sixteen-hour days for weeks on end with no days off, we began another round of internal political maneuvering to be kept on for yet another torturous experience in yet another far-away state.

Persistent, stubborn, and with lots of help from senior staff, I managed to stay in the mix, working for little or no pay in Texas, Michigan, New York, New Jersey, at the Democratic National Convention, and back again in Michigan for the general election. When I finally got around to paying my taxes, I found I had earned $4,500 the entire year! I had seven days off from January 1988 until election night in November. I got by (barely) because the campaign arranged for us to be housed by generous families who often fed us too, and a supporter in Michigan gave me his 1978 Chevette, which helped me get from state to state and made me a more valuable staffer because I had a car.

The campaign was a life-changing experience. I learned more in that one year than in three years at any regular job. The range of skills I developed and honed, the people I met and learned from, the experiences I endured and enjoyed are simply irreplaceable. I made lifelong friends and got hooked by the campaign bug. As brutal and difficult as it often was, I would recommend the experience to any young person.

Networking

After Dukakis's disappointing loss, many of the young staffers descended on Washington, D.C. Out of work, with no place to live, little or no savings, and even less idea of how Washington worked, we simply knew we wanted to work in politics. But Washington was hardly a welcoming place at the time. Dukakis staffers were not in high favor among establishment Democrats, who often blamed us for losing the election to George Bush. The city is always flooded with unemployed campaign workers after an election; having just downsized, few political organizations do any hiring until the next year.

We were several hundred organizers with nothing to do. So we helped each other write resumes and cover letters, traded contacts and job-opening tips, slept on the floors of the few friends who actually had apartments, and organized tons of parties and get-togethers with cheap beer and free hors d'oeuvres.

The young women especially banded together. When we found out about a rare job opening, we would tell each other, feeling that if anyone was to get the job it should be one of us. Vanessa Kirsch and I interviewed for the same job back-to-back and met for lunch afterward to compare notes. When Vanessa got the job, she became

one of our very first employed friends. She got a Capitol Hill apartment, which became a major crash pad for those of us still job
searching.

Although most of my friends were committed to getting jobs in
D.C., I actually wanted to hit the campaign trail again. I had two job
offers for campaigns—one raising money for a U.S. senator seeking
reelection, the other managing the Pittsburgh City Council race of a
man who had never held elected office and was running in the spring
primary against a popular incumbent.

The advice from my friends was nearly unanimous—go work
on the high-profile Senate race! Besides, it would last the entire year.
The Pittsburgh job would end after the May primary, so win or lose
I'd be unemployed in five months. My Iowa boss, Teresa Vilmain,
passed on different advice from top Democratic Party strategist Paul
Tully: a young woman taking a fund-raising job would always be
tracked into fund-raising, but if I became a campaign manager—
even for a dog catcher's race—I could do anything. Within a week
of my arrival in Pittsburgh, the incumbent dropped out, making it
an open seat and bringing four more candidates into the race. We
set fund-raising records and won our five-way primary with over 50
percent of the vote.

Meanwhile, wonderful things were happening back in Washington. Vanessa, Jill Alper, and others organized a potluck dinner for
young Democratic women who were new in town. They invited
friends, who invited friends, and over sixty people showed up at
Vanessa's, bringing with them not only potluck dishes but also little
slips of paper with names and phone numbers of women who
weren't able to come. At the end of the night, they had well over one
hundred names and addresses and a group of women pumped up to
do something. When I returned in May 1989, we had the beginnings
of the Women's Information Network (WIN), an organization to
help young women seeking jobs and political information. We called
it "our answer to the golf course."

Hardcore political organizers with time on our hands, we wrote and mailed a newsletter to our new list, announcing a happy hour where people could bring friends to share drinks and job tips and to exchange resumes. WIN took off. Now it is an established organization serving pro-choice Democratic women both professionally and socially in the D.C. area.

Just as many adults contributed to the success of STOP Nuclear War without taking it over, WIN became a success thanks in large part to the generous support of established Washington Democratic women like Karen Mulhauser. She was our mentor and fairy godmother at every turn, housing our volunteers, advising our elected leadership, and drawing us maps of Washington's ever-changing political landscape. WIN became a way for successful women to reach back and help newcomers along.

In 1990, WIN hosted its first Women Opening Doors for Women (WODW) event; it was kicked off with a major reception, followed by small dinner parties in beautiful homes. Each dinner party featured four Women of Achievement, women who were successful in certain areas of Democratic politics: in campaigns, on Capitol Hill, in nonprofit organizations, as lobbyists or political consultants. Up to twenty young women interested in that field of work attended each dinner; they got advice, ideas, and the "inside scoop" on how to break into, and ultimately succeed in, the area of politics that most interested them.

To organize our first WODW, WIN members asked their bosses, their bosses' friends, and anyone else they could find either to host a dinner, be a special guest, or help fund the program. The first WODW was a resounding success; now it is an annual event with over twenty separate dinner parties and six hundred young women participating.

In the midst of getting WIN off the ground, I went to New Jersey to manage two state assembly races. In December 1989, physically and emotionally exhausted from living out of my car trunk, eating pizza and donuts, and never having enough sleep, I decided to spend a year in Washington, get a "real" job, and rest up for 1990, when I planned to manage a race for the U.S. Congress.

I returned to D.C., slept on my friends' floors, and searched for work. I accepted a job in a small direct-mail firm, even though I had absolutely no interest in direct mail or fund-raising. But most of the interview with my future boss at the direct-mail firm was spent laughing—about politics, campaign life, and regular life. Two packed years in politics had taught me that you really have to like and respect the people you work with in this business. Politics is never a nine-to-five job. It is always intense, and at some level it always becomes personal.

Anyone who has worked on campaigns and knows from the inside how stressful and crazy they are will not be surprised that I decided a boss with an easy laugh who understood campaigns inside and out was the best fit for me. I stayed there for more than three years until moving over to the Women's Campaign Fund (WCF) in 1993.

There are many choices and paths in politics. My job at the WCF was ideal—I was helping pro-choice women candidates of both parties run for and win elected office. When it was time to leave, what could possibly hold my interest? Realizing how much I loved my job made me want to choose a career that would always be interesting, challenging, and rewarding, so I decided to pursue public opinion research. It would also allow me to continue my work in the nonprofit and campaign worlds, merging my commitment to social change with my everyday work.

Once I made the decision to go into polling, my life took one of its usual turns, and in 1996, I left the Women's Campaign Fund not for polling but to be the political director of the National Jewish Democratic Council (NJDC). NJDC is a grassroots membership organization working to promote issues of importance to the Jewish community, including support for Israel, separation of church and state, and a woman's right to choose.

After 1996 and another demanding and intense election cycle, I started to think about my mother again, and realized that if I was ever to become a pollster, it was time to make the switch. In 1997, I joined the polling firm of Bennett, Petts, and Blumenthal as a vice president.

I never left town to manage a congressional race as I had planned. Washington has grown on me over the years. It can be a tough, even cruel place professionally. Close friends and former associates are blackballed, investigated, and sometimes just trashed. Over time, you develop a thicker skin and sort out your real friends from those who are simply acquaintances of convenience.

No formal credentials are required to be a success in politics. The down side is that your reputation is everything; a tarnished reputation can severely damage your ability to earn a living. The plus side is that the nation's capital is filled with people who care deeply about their work, are dedicated to making the world a better place, and continually reinvent their own visions of how they can best make a difference. People are engaged in their work with a level of commitment very rare outside the field of social change and politics.

Since my early childhood, watching my mother pick up trash while taking a walk, seeing her develop a conservation curriculum for elementary school children, and cherishing her fierce defense of me when things got tough, I have come to believe that each person possesses the power to change the world through her own choices and actions.

Every time I donate blood, volunteer at my local farmers market, or show up at an abortion clinic at 5:00 A.M. on a winter's morning to escort women safely inside, I am reminded of the power of one person to make a difference. When a system is unjust and the things you value most are attacked, you can, in your own way, find a way to fight back.

In Hebrew, *tikkun olam* means "to heal the world." Judaism teaches that healing the world is one of our highest obligations. I never knew the Hebrew phrase growing up; as an adult, those words serve as a framework for the decisions I make about my life. If I learned anything from my mother, it is this: life is meant to be lived fully, and if you do nothing else, you should try to make the world a better place than it was when you entered it.

VICKI MILES-LAGRANGE is a United States district judge for
the Western District of Oklahoma, the first African American
federal judge in the six states that make up the Tenth Circuit.
She has served in all three branches of government. She was
the first woman United States attorney in Oklahoma. In 1986,
she was elected as the first African American woman in the
Oklahoma state senate, where she served until 1993. She formerly chaired the law and justice committee of the National
Conference of State Legislators. She serves as deaconess and
usher in her local church where she also plays cello in the or-
chestra. Miles-LaGrange is a trustee of her alma mater Vassar
College and holds a J.D. degree from Howard University and
an honorary doctor of laws degree from Oklahoma City University School of Law.

Building Bridges

VICKI MILES-LAGRANGE

A BRIDGE IS A STRUCTURE that crosses and provides passage over an obstacle. To build a bridge, one must span two points separated by distance. How do we build bridges between people of different races, different nationalities, different backgrounds, different economic circumstances, different political philosophies, and different interests?

As we approach the next millennium, it is important to realize that our diversity gives this nation an extraordinary advantage. Our America of united states is made up of people with all kinds of faces, from all kinds of places. If we build bridges, the faces of America's people are our greatest opportunity; if we build walls, those faces become our greatest challenge.

America is the guardian of each citizen and should govern with compassion. Lady Liberty stands in New York harbor as the cornerstone of hope for all of America's diverse inhabitants. Diversity should truly be a vital thread in the fabric of America. It should not be an attempt to blend the differences—to make them look the same or be the same—because individual experiences may vary because of race, culture, ethnicity, religion, or other reasons.

Diversity does not mean just sitting next to someone who is different. It is much more than that. Diversity is an inclusive outlook that enables Americans to consider different people as assets, not as liabilities. This kind of diversity creates an environment where America's people honestly believe their differences are valued and that they, too, can sing "America." Diversity is strength.

Each of us is a product of her own environment and a product of her experiences. I learned to negotiate different worlds at an early age. The issue of race probably played the biggest part in shaping my experiences and transforming my humanity. I had no idea that I was limited by anything other than my own imagination.

As a child I always loved to travel from my home in Oklahoma City across the many miles and states of the "Deep South" to my grandparents' home in Buford, Georgia. Today, with the modern highways and interstates, we think very little about traveling across the country. However, in the times of my memory, the roads were two-lane, twisting and winding over hills and through valleys. Roads were sheltered from sight by trees and vegetation where anything might happen to a small black family traveling alone. Concerned about his family's safety, my father would call ahead to relatives to get the informal Klan Watch.

It is now the end of last decade of the twentieth century—almost forty years from those cross-country treks of my childhood. We are on the threshold of the twenty-first century, yet probably no rational American can be comfortable with where we are on issues of intolerance, indifference, and prejudice. As a nation we have not yet fully exploited our extraordinary wealth of human talent. Nor have we completely captured the strength of America's diversity to the greatest extent possible.

Lessons in Love

Daily reminders of the color of my skin, albeit subtle and seemingly insignificant, somehow force me to call upon my inner strength, my personal commitment to excellence, and to renew my faith. My parents provided me the necessary ammunition to deflect the "isms" (racism, sexism, classism) through their quiet vigilance and broad vision. They taught me lessons in working hard, being honest, having integrity, not sweating the small stuff, and keeping your best foot forward. If nothing else they always gave me enough hope for the future. More important, they taught me not to hate. Children are not born hating—it is a learned emotion.

In a speech the legendary A. Philip Randolph gave in 1961 to the Negro American Labor Council, he said that men often hate each other because they fear each other; they fear each other because they do not know each other; they do not know each other because they cannot communicate; they cannot communicate because they are separated.

Early on I was intrigued by these matters of love, hate, and color. I was raised in the Baptist Church and during my formative years I could always count on seeing and hearing Dr. Martin Luther King Jr. every year at the Progressive National Baptist Convention.

Oh, if I could just paint you a picture of the excitement, when late in August each year I would be allowed to tag along with my elder cousin, Luella Dunn, on a charter bus across America to the place of that year's convention. What an unforgettable experience it was! Momma would pack Cousin Luella and me a wonderful bag of food, hoping it would last for a large part of the trip to help defray expenses.

My friend Angela (now Angela Monson, Oklahoma state senator) and I were the only children on the bus, and we were doted on by all the older church members. Besides my momma's mouth-watering fried chicken and home-canned bread-and-butter pickles, we could always count on being plied with food from the other sojourners on the bus. To make time pass, the group would sing all the old spirituals and hymns—the men singing the low parts and the women the high, and from time to time someone would really catch the spirit and sing out on his or her own.

But as memorable as the bus trip was, nothing could compare to getting finally to our destination and being a part of the convention. Through a child's eyes, Dr. King was larger than life. He was always talking about overcoming something and loving your neighbor. Although I was just a child, I knew that Dr. King was talking to me. His words and the scenes from those countless conventions long ago became indelibly carved into my memory.

Whether at the convention or on the six o'clock evening news that my family usually watched during dinner, it seemed Dr. King was always marching around with lots of people and praying and proclaiming expressions of hope. Sometimes on the news I saw people who looked like me being squirted with water hoses or being held back by policemen with big dogs. I didn't understand why.

I could not process my observations and impressions of those mean-spirited people. I did not understand why those people who looked like my family were so hated. I distinctly remember, however, those scenes being aborted a time or two by my parents' abruptly turning off the television set. I remember my questions and my natural curiosity being answered by my parents' unnatural silence. I remember their occasional change of subjects. My own childish inattention quickly dissipated any further interest in receiving an answer.

Both of my parents were then public school teachers in Oklahoma. For them education was a lifelong pursuit that was interrupted only by death. Learning was the most important thing we did together except maybe dinner and prayer. Questions were always welcome and never seemed awkward. No question was dumb if you did not know the answer. No question in the Miles house ever went unanswered, except at those peculiar times when I made precocious inquiries about race and intolerance. Silence was probably the only means they knew to reconcile the pain of the blatant racism of the 1960s and at the same time keep our attitudes positive.

The Governor

My most memorable lesson in love came during the summer of 1970. The pain and the disappointment was permanently etched onto the consciousness of a sixteen-year-old. It would hurt for a long time. My parents were not silent this time. They forced me to face an incomprehensible experience. They shepherded me through it with a spirit of love and reconciliation. The importance of diversity was intensely magnified. That bad bout with one of those "isms" would forever shape the way I, as one human being, would confront and cope with the intolerance of race discrimination.

The experience was bittersweet. I was selected to represent Bishop McGuinness High School, whose student body at that time was mostly white, at the 1970 Oklahoma Girls State, sponsored by the American Legion. The selection criteria for representation to Girls State described a girl who exemplified character, courage, service, companionship and scholarship, and other qualities that are necessary to the preservation and protection of the fundamental institutions of our government and the advancement of society.

Four hundred and sixteen girls—eight of them black—came from across Oklahoma to learn how state government worked through a hands-on experience of running a mock government. This was an unbelievable opportunity for a young girl whose passion had been social studies since the second grade.

My mind reflected on a letter I had written to President John F. Kennedy in 1961 congratulating him on his election. I shared with him my excitement about serving my country. I still have the response I received. This correspondence, along with President Kennedy's famous words of his inaugural address, "Ask not what your country can do for you, ask what you can do for your country," served as a catalyst for a seven-year-old "Negro" girl. I truly believed America is for everyone; that everyone has a responsibility to participate, and everyone can realize her dreams.

At Girls State, out of the four hundred and sixteen girls, one was elected by her peers to be "governor." Traditionally, the girl elected governor would represent the state of Oklahoma at Girls Nation. Girls campaigned for election just as in a regular election. What fun it was, and what wonderful friends I made! The day of the election finally came and everyone was full of excitement and anticipation. Voting machines were used that year for the first time in the history of Oklahoma Girls State.

You can imagine my elation when my name was announced as winner of the Oklahoma Girls State governorship. Not only was I elected to be governor of Girls State but I fully expected to represent my state at Girls Nation as had been the tradition.

The night before the awaited Girls Nation announcement, my rightful expectations were extinguished by a reality check from my junior counselor. She compassionately tried to ease my hurt and piercing rejection. The Girls State counselor informed me that a controversial decision had been made during an all-night meeting. The decision was to send the girl I defeated for the office of governor to Girls Nation. The decision was made not to send me to represent Oklahoma because I was a "Negro."

My parents, along with many other parents, were in Ada early the next day to retrieve their daughter. I was sad and hurt, but relieved to see them. The governor was packed and ready to go home. The governor had no desire or intention of attending the closing ceremony.

My father, of course, had another plan for the governor. He told me that he understood my disappointment. In his usual few words, Daddy reminded me that my peers elected me governor and that I would attend the closing ceremony. He further assured me that I would be gracious and congratulate the Girls Nation victor with genuineness.

This was the greatest lesson I ever learned about racism, about the dignity of losing, and about what can happen when fear, ignorance, and prejudice prevail. My sheltered upbringing had blinded me to any notion that prejudice in all its ugliness would ever appear in certain places, especially in the halls of government—or in this instance, a mock government. A government of the people, by the people, and for the people. My passion for government and history had intensified and I was determined to right what I believed to be genuine racism by confronting it wherever I saw it, with an unbroken spirit and an attitude of love.

My silent rage broadened my thinking. It made me question whether anyone cared enough to extend the privileges of democracy and heal ourselves and our fellow man. My parents helped me to channel my anger positively. I replayed the events over and over again in my mind. I kept saying to myself that we must renew our collective commitment to fairness, justice, equal rights, and equal opportunity for all Americans. I clearly understood that freedom and justice would never be theoretical concepts for me. Rather, I would seek each with vigor, and continue to share the joy, the creativity, and the progress that are the products of freedom.

A Divided Nation

By the time I entered Vassar College I was committed to a study of political science and black studies. Up until that time my academic experiences were devoid of any perspective that included the history of my people. The language of the Declaration of Independence took on a new meaning for me: "We hold these truths to be self-evident, that all men are created equal, that they are endowed by their Creator with certain inalienable rights, that among these are life, liberty and the pursuit of happiness."

I paused when I first read that our preeminent and brilliant statesman Thomas Jefferson had written (in *Notes on the State of*

Virginia, 1782) that blacks were inferior to whites "in the endow-
ments both of body and mind." I mourned when I first understood
that the great principles of political freedom and of natural justice
embodied in the Declaration of Independence as well as in the Constitution did not extend to people like me or to my ancestors.

The designers of our great republic, even though there was no
specific reference to the word "slave" in the Constitution, for example, counted slaves as three-fifths of a person for white representation in the House of Representatives, obligated states to return
runaway slaves to their owner, and denied indentured servants the
protection of the privileges and immunities clause, which was limited to citizens. The soul of America was ripped apart by that peculiar institution of slavery. Our nation remained divided in its efforts
to abolish it. Slavery had been sanctioned and institutionalized by
the legislative branch of our government.

A reaffirmation of slavery was given by the judicial branch of
our American government in 1857. In *Dred Scott* v. *Sanford,* the
United States Supreme Court sanctioned the denial of rights of both
freemen and slaves. The Court ruled that people of African descent
were not and could not be citizens of the United States, could not
sue in any of the United States courts, and had no rights under the
Constitution of the United States. Chief Justice Roger Brooke Taney,
writing for the majority, said blacks were of an "inferior order" and
"so far inferior, that they had no rights which the white man was
bound to respect."

Passage of the Civil War Amendments, the thirteenth, fourteenth,
and fifteenth to the United States Constitution, represented a tangible
political gain for people of African descent. The Thirteenth Amendment freed the slaves, the Fourteenth Amendment granted the rights
of citizenship to blacks, and the Fifteenth Amendment gave blacks
the right to vote. Many Southern states, however, enacted Black
Codes as a direct attempt to circumvent the Fourteenth and Fifteenth
Amendments. For example, many Southern states circumvented the

Fifteenth Amendment by instituting poll taxes or "grandfather clauses," which allowed an individual to vote only if his ancestors had enjoyed the right to vote as of January 1, 1866. The effect was to eliminate many blacks from the voting rolls.

In 1896, the United States Supreme Court in *Plessy v. Ferguson* institutionalized segregation in the fabric of American life through the doctrine of "separate but equal." This doctrine dominated the American legal system and way of life for the next half century. *De facto* and *de jure* segregation were the norm. "Jim Crow" laws were the rule. "Separate but unequal" was the reality in separate schools for whites and blacks, segregated public accommodations, transportation, and housing. Justice Harlan in his dissent in the *Plessy* case said, "the destinies of the two races, in this country, are indissolubly linked together, and the interests of both require that the common government of all shall not permit the seeds of race hatred to be planted under the sanction of law."

Ada Lois Sipuel's Challenge

During the late 1940s and early 1950s, a chipping away of the separate but equal doctrine was commenced through a series of court battles. In 1948, in my native Oklahoma, a black woman applicant, qualified in all respects, battled all the way to the United States Supreme Court to win the right to attend Oklahoma's state-supported law school.

In *Sipuel v. University of Oklahoma Board of Regents*, Ada Lois Sipuel, an honor graduate of Langston University, a historically black college, was refused admission to the University of Oklahoma College of Law because she was a "Negro." The Supreme Court disagreed and ordered the state to provide her a legal education. University officials, trying to comply with the Court's directive and at the same time enforce the separate but equal doctrine, created the Langston University Law School. The school consisted of a single room at the Oklahoma state capital and had one student, Ada Lois Sipuel. The Court eventually found this remedy unacceptable and ordered Sipuel admitted to the University of Oklahoma College of Law. Sipuel's lawyer was Thurgood Marshall, who later became a justice of the United States Supreme Court. Marshall sued again on behalf of another client, George W. McLaurin, and forced the University of Oklahoma to integrate all of its graduate schools.

In 1954, in *Brown* v. *Board of Education of Topeka,* the United States Supreme Court overturned *Plessy's* separate but equal doctrine. Chief Justice Earl Warren, writing for the majority, said, "we conclude that in the field of public education the doctrine of separate but equal has no place." The Court ruled that the intentional segregation of African American children in public schools was a violation of the equal protection clause of the United States Constitution. "To separate them [black children] from others of similar age and qualifications solely because of their race generates a feeling of inferiority as to their status in the community that may affect their hearts and minds in a way unlikely ever to be undone."

Brown signaled the first time in American history that the "inalienable rights" referred to in the United States Constitution were guaranteed, as a matter of law, to Americans of African descent.

A Bridge to the Future

The goal of an excellent education is critical to America's ability to build bridges through diversity. The future prosperity of our nation cannot be guaranteed unless we educate our children and build bridges through our diversity. Without a good education from the beginning, America will never close its methamphetamine labs of suburban America, its crack cocaine houses of the inner city, and its marijuana fields of rural America. Thomas Jefferson summed it up best: "let us in education dream of an aristocracy of achievement rising out of a democracy of opportunity."

Some critics argue that any notion of building bridges through diversity is flawed because we cannot go far enough without infringing on the rights of others. Where would we be as a nation today if our founding fathers had not pursued their vision of the Constitution and of the Declaration of Independence because they didn't go far enough? Where would we be as a nation today if Franklin D. Roosevelt had not pursued his vision of a New Deal because it didn't go far enough? If John F. Kennedy had not pursued his vision to put an American on the moon because his space efforts didn't go far enough? If Martin Luther King Jr. had not pursued his vision of nonviolent social change because it didn't go far enough?

I truly believe that America's people are this country's greatest resource. Indeed, the future of our American community depends upon investing in our people. I believe most of us share a commitment to peace, excellence, and human liberty. The best hope for our community lies in education, and the best hope for our states and our nation lies in cooperation and coexistence.

Coupled with the qualities of freedom and equality are the rights of America's men, women, and children. For those same rights, the founding fathers, as well as our ancestors, fought to forge and preserve our nation. For those same rights, Abraham Lincoln issued the Emancipation Proclamation, Congressman John Mercer Langston sought excellence in higher education and disproved the vicious rumor that black legislators during the Reconstruction were illiterate, a tired Rosa Parks refused to give up her seat and move to the back of a crowded bus, and Martin Luther King Jr. challenged America to pay more than lip service to the admonition of John Locke that indeed all human beings are created equal.

As a nation, the choice is ours to commit to the preservation of the dignity of the human condition in our society. The choice is ours to commit to the integrity of our system, to peace with justice within our communities, and to a social environment wherein our children can grow and learn and develop and become useful citizens in our community. The choice is ours to demand community peace, like national peace, which requires mutual respect. We must extend respect to our neighbors, but we also have the right to expect it in return.

To recall the truths of A. Philip Randolph, we will not hate each other if we do not fear each other. We will not fear each other if we know each other. We will not know each other unless we communicate. We cannot communicate if we are separated.

The choice of America on the eve of the next millennium is whether we dwell on the things that make us different or lift up the things we share in common—the things that make us one—a sort of transcendent humanity. The choice is ours as a nation: to build bridges through inclusion or to remain on the shores of separation as the new millennium passes us by.

THE EDITOR

ᕱ

N ANCY M. NEUMAN was national president of the League of
Women Voters from 1986 to 1990. A lecturer and writer on
women in politics and public policy, she is a former distinguished
visiting professor at Washington and Jefferson College (1991 and
1994), Bucknell University (1992), and Pomona College (1990). She
has been a Woodrow Wilson Visiting Fellow since 1992. Neuman
earned a B.A. degree from Pomona College and an M.A. degree in
political science from the University of California at Berkeley. She
holds honorary degrees from Pomona College and Westminster
College.

She is the editor of *A Voice of Our Own: Leading American
Women Celebrate the Right to Vote* (1996) and author of *The
League of Women Voters in Perspective: 1920–1995* (1994) and
the discussion guide for the award-winning documentary film
Mr. Justice Brennan (1996).

She is a director and past president (1992–1996) of the Pennsylvania Women's Campaign Fund. A public member of the American
Bar Association Council of the Section of Legal Education, she served
on the Disciplinary Board of the Pennsylvania Supreme Court and
the Pennsylvania Judicial Inquiry and Review Board and Federal Judicial Nominating Commission. Active in housing policy and civil
rights, she is an officer and former president of the Housing Assistance Council, a former director of the Pennsylvania Housing Finance Agency, the Federal Home Loan Bank of Pittsburgh, and the

Leadership Conference on Civil Rights. She received the Distinguished Daughter of Pennsylvania award in 1987.

A former president of her state and local Leagues of Women Voters, Neuman chaired the league's national Equal Rights Amendment ratification campaign for three years.

INDEX

❦

Farmers, African American, 83–85
Feinstein, D., 52
Felton, R., 50
Feminism: journeys to, 25–32, 207.
See also Politics and organizing
Ferguson, Plessy v., 225
Finney, J., 123
Firearms dealers, federally licensed, 116
First woman: across the Arctic, 6–7;
African American federal judge in
the Tenth Circuit, 216; African
American state senator in Okla-
homa, 216; African American U.S.
Congresswoman, 51; African
American U.S. Congresswoman
from North Carolina, 80; African
American U.S. Senator, 51, 100;
Asian American U.S. Congress-
woman, 51; elected governor in her
own right, 123; the experience of
being a, 101–102; governor of
New Jersey, 130; governor of Oregon, 122, 128; Greek American
U.S. Senator, 58; Latina at NPR in
Washington, D.C., 194; lieutenant
governor of Maryland, 97; Mexican American state representative,
163; Mexican American state senate leader, 154; on the Minnesota
Supreme Court, 38; non-elected
state governor, 124; pregnant state
legislator, 164; Secretary of State,
52, 98; state attorney general of
New Jersey, 130; state house majority leader, 127; state supreme
court justice of New Jersey, 130; in
the U.S. Congress, 171; in the U.S.
Senate, 50
First women's groups or organizations: national, 50, 69–79; to the

South Pole, 7–9; working for
women's suffrage, 47–48. See also
Statistics
Flexible working hours, 161, 176, 177
Florio, J., 132
Food stamp benefits, 86
Ford Foundation, 159–160
Ford, G., 28, 115
Foremothers, our, 47–49, 87,
183–184; the legacy of, 37–38,
102–103
Frank, A., 11–12
Freedom: of information, 49; women's
reproductive, 31–32, 66–67, 212
Freeze, nuclear, 206
Friedan, B., 95
Friends, the Society of (Quakers), 82
Fund-raising jobs, 211
Fuster, J. B., 68

G
Gallegos, H., 160
Gangs, reporting about, 194–195
Gardebring, S., 42
Gender gap: in earnings, 71, 106; in
elective office, 51, 97–98, 108; in
voting, 49, 51–52, 174–176; and
what women want, 176–178, 179.
See also Statistics
Gender, and public service, 46–47,
94, 164. See also First woman
General Services Administration
(GSA), 167
Genetic research, 64–65; and discrim-
ination, 65–66
Girls Nation, 221–223
"Gloria Steinem of the Republican
Party," 29
Gore, A., 144, 145, 146–148, 149,
151

Photography Credits